A TRAGEDY REVEALED

ARRIGO PETACCO

A Tragedy Revealed

The Story of the Italian Population
of Istria, Dalmatia, and
Venezia Giulia, 1943–1956

Translated by Konrad Eisenbichler

UNIVERSITY OF TORONTO PRESS
Toronto Buffalo London

© University of Toronto Press Incorporated 2005
Toronto Buffalo London
Printed in Canada

ISBN 0-8020-3921-9

*A Tragedy Revealed: The Story of the Italian Population of Istria, Dalmatia, and Venezia Giulia,
1943–1956* is a translation of *L'esodo: la tragedia negata degli italiani d'Istria, Dalmazia e
Venezia Giulia* (Milan: Arnoldo Mondadori Editore SpA, 1999)

Toronto Italian Studies

Printed on acid-free paper

Library and Archives Canada Cataloguing in Publication

Petacco, Arrigo
A tragedy revealed : the story of the Italian population of Istria, Dalmatia, and Venezia
Giulia, 1943–1956 / Arrigo Petacco ; translated by Konrad Eisenbichler

(Toronto Italian studies)
Translation of: L'esodo.
Includes bibliographical references and index.
ISBN 0-8020-3921-9

1. Italians – Istria (Croatia and Slovenia) – History – 20th century.   2. Italians – Croatia –
Dalmatia – History – 20th century.   3. World War, 1939–1945 – Territorial questions –
Italy. 4. World War, 1939–1945 – Territorial questions – Yugoslavia. 5. Istria (Croatia and
Slovenia) – History – 20th century.   6. Dalmatia (Croatia – History – 20th century.
7. Friuli-Venezia Giulia (Italy) – History – 20th century.   8. Venezia Giulia (Territory
under Allied occupation, 1945–1947) – Politics and government.   I. Eisenbichler,
Konrad   II. Title.   III. Series.

DR1350.I78P4713 2005   949.72'00451   C2004-906132-1

University of Toronto Press acknowledges the financial assistance to its publishing
program of the Canada Council for the Arts and the Ontario Arts Council.

University of Toronto Press acknowledges the financial support for its
publishing activities of the Government of Canada through the
Book Publishing Industry Development Program (BPIDP).

This translation is published with the financial assistance of the
Club Giuliano Dalmato di Toronto.

This volume has been translated and is being published in commemoration
of the fiftieth anniversary of the arrival in Canada
of the first Italian refugees from Venezia Giulia, Istria, and Dalmatia,
1951–2001

Contents

3. Goodbye Istria   109

Translator's Preface

Until recently, a great silence lay over one of the most wrenching human tragedies of modern Italy. Although thousands if not millions of Italians were aware of it, hardly anyone dared mention it, let alone speak openly about it. From the government to the media, from the cultural elite to the common citizen, a self-imposed silence ensured that the harsh reality of what happened in four Italian provinces during and after the Second World War would remain forever tucked away, hidden, perhaps even forgotten in one of those dusty corners of history that, for the sake of personal and national sanity, are best left untouched and unexplored. Only a few individuals had the nerve, or the courage, to scream out the awful word that had come to encapsulate all their pain and anger: *foibe*! I first heard it like that, screamed in anger by a flag-waving Italian standing in front of an Italian cultural centre in Toronto, Canada. She then screamed it again indoors, disrupting the celebrations being hosted by an Italian social club. I understood then that something profoundly tragic and painful lay behind that word, that gesture, that anger. I had a suspicion, but I did not understand the horror of the reality it contained. That was back in 1991.

By the middle of that decade, things in Italy had begun to change. The traditional political parties were disintegrating, the government was changing, and the media were beginning to pay attention to the old folk waving old flags and to the various associations of Italian refugees keeping alive their various stories. The wartime history of Italy's eastern border had suddenly become front-page news. Some of the old-guard Italian Communists tried to paint this new interest in the stories of the Italian refugees and in the atrocities perpetrated by Marshal Tito's Communists as yet another attempt by diehard Fascists to resurrect their long-dead nationalist and irridentist designs, but the truth was out – Yugoslavian Communists had carried out a genocide and a forced evacuation of Italians from Dalmatia, Istria, and Venezia Giulia of biblical proportions and this tragedy reverberated deeply with recent events in Serbia and in Kosovo. Fifty years had passed, and many of the participants were dead, but the survivors were telling stories that sent a shiver down the collective spine of Italians on the peninsula. Some of the old folk, most of them well over seventy, remembered. But the younger generations knew nothing about it. Italian textbooks and school-teachers had studiously avoided telling them how, in the 1940s, Italy lost four provinces to Yugoslavia and how an entire people had lost their homes, their lands, and many of them their lives only because they were Italian.

With the sudden interest in this tragedy, one book caught the imagination of Italian readers: Arrigo Petacco's *L'esodo: la tragedia negata degli italiani d'Istria, Dalmazia e Venezia Giulia*, first published by Mondadori, in Milan, in 1999. This was not a detached, scholarly examination of a vexed historical question, as might come from the pen of an eminent university professor – had it been so, few would have read it and its impact would have been limited to a few ripples within a confined academic circle of 'experts.' This, instead, was a book of 'popular history' written by an eminent journalist with clear although perhaps academically unorthodox ideas about writing history. He used a language that reached out and spoke directly to the reader. Petacco's intention here, as in his other books, was to chronicle, to tell a story, to dig up the dirt and expose it in the best tradition of investigative journalism. As he himself explains on his own website (www.arrigopetacco.net), his goal is investigative journalism and the telling of a good story: 'I consider my books to be very long news reports, 300 pages long, not 30.' 'I am an investigator of history. For many years I was a journalist, and I even had some scoops in my youth.Then, at a certain point, I discovered history.' 'My work is to resolve the mysteries of history. Mystery is what attracts me the most.' 'I became interested in history when working at the RAI [the Italian national radio and television network]. What was my first discovery? That everything I had read and studied in my school textbooks was wrong, false, and dreamt up.' 'I am grateful to historians because they have left behind so many black holes for me to plug with my books. I have turned upside down truths that have always been deemed unassailable.' 'I think like a chronicler of history. I try to write fluently and to be understood.' 'A historian who writes a book of history keeps his most careerist colleague in mind, but I keep in mind the least educated of my readers. This is the difference.'

By the time *L'esodo* appeared in 1999, Petacco had had a career many experienced journalists would have envied. He enjoyed an enormous national reputation and could claim a long list of distinguished achievements in print as well as on the screen. Born in 1929 in the small town of Castelnuovo Magra (in the province of La Spezia, the southernmost corner of Liguria, on the Italian Riviera), he began working at the age of seventeen for Sandro Pertini (the future president of Italy) at the Socialist newspaper *Il lavoro nuovo*. On his web page, Petacco recalls this first job, not without a hint of irony:

> When I was seventeen I went to work in a newspaper and there I did my university. It was the *Lavoro nuovo* [New Labour], directed by Sandro Pertini, a Genoese newspaper, Socialist, during Fascism it had become a bit Fascist, but then returned to its roots. One day I asked Pertini: 'Why am I paid only half a salary and the others a full salary?' He answered: 'Because we are comrades, Socialists.' Whatever the case, I learned my profession there.

He certainly did, for he quickly rose through the ranks to become not only a journalist and special correspondent for several newspapers and magazines (*Grazia, Epoca, Panorama, Corriere della Sera, Il Tempo, Il Resto del Carlino*), but also editor of the Milanese periodical *Storia illustrata* and of the Florentine daily *La Nazione*, one of Italy's most prestigious and respected newspapers. While working for the RAI, Petacco produced several successful television programs and films, including a four-part mini series on Giuseppe Garibaldi. He has also written four film scripts, one of them drawn from his own *Il prefetto di ferro* (The Iron Prefect), starring Giuliano Gemma, Claudia Cardinale, and Stefano Satta Flores. A prolific author, with more than two dozen titles published by major Italian houses – Mondadori, Rizzoli, Laterza, De Agostini – Petacco is not afraid to tackle difficult subjects and, when necessary, to overturn generally held 'truths.'

And this is what *L'esodo* did. It exposed a wound that had been festering in Italy's postwar psyche and challenged long-held views of how deep that wound was and who had inflicted it. Not surprisingly, the book was awarded the prestigious Premio Acqui Storia for the best work of popular history. The prize jury noted that Petacco had carried out a massive amount of work on original archival documents and in doing so had brought to light many details about the tragedy of the *foibe*. Because of Petacco and others like him, the word *foibe* has now officially been given a second meaning: the *Garzantina*, the most widely used Italian encyclopaedia, no longer defines the word simply as 'a type of sink-hole found in Istria.' It has added this important sentence: 'Between 1943 and 1945 they were the site of massacres of Italians (from 5,000 to 10,000, according to estimates) carried out by the partisan troops of Marshal Tito.' Many Italian schoolbooks have followed suit by briefly discussing these tragic events in their accounts of the Second World War and its aftermath. A number of municipal governments in Italy – Assisi, Bari, Brindisi, Florence, Palermo, Rome, and Vicenza, to name just a few – have renamed a city street or a piazza in honour of the 'Martyrs of the *foibe*.' These urban markers have been planted beside street names such as via Fiume, via Pola, via Zara, and so on, many of which were in place even before the war. Finally, the Italian government has recently decreed 10 February, the anniversary of the Italian exodus from Pola, to be a national day of remembrance for those Italians who died in the *foibe*. In short, Italy is reopening one of the most agonizing pages of its recent history and is trying to come to terms with it.

Scholarship, unfortunately, has not yet done the same. A number of popular histories, personal memoirs, and party-line descriptions of the events of the Second World War along the eastern border of Italy have been published (especially in Trieste), yet there is still no scholarly text that does justice to the fate of the people of Gorizia, Trieste, Pola, Fiume, Zara, and hundreds of smaller towns who suffered at the hands of Tito's Communists and who paid, with their homes and many with their lives, for the disastrous errors of Fascist Italy. Here, the academy is lagging behind the press, the people, and even the government.

English-language scholarship is lagging still farther behind. It lacks even the 'popular histories' exemplified so well by Petacco's book and by the 'personal histories' written by so many survivors of those events. In the 1950s, many refugees exiled themselves yet again, emigrating from Italy to other parts of Europe, to the Americas, to South Africa, even to Australia. The situation on the Italian peninsula was such that they simply could not stay. Having abandoned their homes in order to remain Italian, they were obliged to abandon Italy in order to rebuild their lives. Attempts have been made to document some of their experiences, but more must be done before we can fully understand the story of Trieste, Istria, and Dalmatia. Perhaps this translation of Petacco's moving narrative will inspire a young doctoral candidate at an English-speaking university, or an older, well-established historian, to carry out scholarly work in this area and introduce the events to the Anglo-American academic world.

In translating this work, I have tried to retain as much as possible the conversational, easygoing tone of Petacco's original prose. This is a narrative, not a scholarly work. This book tells a story, and so its language rises and falls as would the voice of an old man recounting the events of his past – at times joyfully, at other times mournfully, at times with admiration, at other times with bitterness. I have added very few footnotes to help the English reader who is not conversant with Italian history. I have avoided footnotes whenever possible so as not to turn Petacco's work into what he never intended it to be: a thoroughly referenced academic history. The author did provide a bibliography, and so I have included it at the end of the volume, as he did. But I have made no attempt to reference the narrative to these books – such an effort would have been a Herculean if not a Sisyphean task. For exactly the same reason, I have not tried to locate and transcribe citations and references that were originally in English and that were translated (or paraphrased) by the author into Italian; I have simply translated the author's Italian back into English and left it at that.

Because the work was originally in Italian and talks about cities and places that were Italian at the time in question, I have retained the Italian form of their names out of respect for their history: Pola (not Pula), Fiume (not Rijeka), Capodistria (not Koper), and so on.

In translating this book, I have incurred a number of debts that I will never be able to repay, but which I am eager to acknowledge. First and foremost, I must thank Guido Braini, who first directed me to Petacco's work and asked me to translate it. His suggestion was supported by many of my Giuliano-Dalmati friends, first among them the recently departed Alceo Lini, and later by Dario Rinaldi, president of the Associazione Giuliani nel Mondo (Trieste); Silvio Delbello, president of the Unione degli Istriani (Trieste); Marina Petronio, herself a published chronicler of Istrian and Dalmatian expatriates; and Rosanna Giuricin, an indefatigable journalist and narrator originally from Rovigno but now working in Trieste. Their support found a catalyst in dott. Bruno Fulvio Castelli, who sent me a copy of Petacco's book as a gift after we had spoken about it in Peschiera del Garda. In his accompanying letter,

Castelli wrote: 'Spero che ti interessi' ('I hope it will be of interest for you') – what an understatement! Once I began reading it, I could not put it down.

In the course of the work I was lucky to have friends and colleagues to help me resolve the inevitable cruxes: Sandra Parmegiani, of the University of Western Ontario, and Anne Urbancic and Manuela Scarci, both of the University of Toronto, were indispensable as linguists, colleagues, and friends. In assiduous e-mail conversations, Fulvio Percovich (in Uruguay) and Giulio Scala (in Italy) tackled questions that only refugees who lived through those years could answer.

I completed the first draft of this translation in the course of a very pleasant and productive term as a Visiting Professor in the Department of Spanish, Italian, and Portuguese at the University of Virginia (Charlottesville). I am grateful to that university and to my colleagues there for the peaceful setting they provided, not to mention the intellectual stimulation. I was fortunate to have had Donald L. Shaw as my colleague in Virginia and to have met his brother Kenneth Edwin Shaw, briefly visiting from England. Their experiences in the British armed forces during the Second World War helped me better understand some of the events and tensions described by Petacco and translate more accurately some of the military terms. In the early stages of the project, Anna Chiafele was a cheerful and ready sounding board for my linguistic uncertainties.

I wish to acknowledge the support of the Club Giuliano-Dalmato di Toronto, a social club for Istriani, Giuliani, Fiumani, and Dalmati of Italian extraction living in the Toronto area. They have provided me with a human context for the story told in this book and with many, many hours of pleasant companionship.

My parents, Erich and Ivetta Eisenbichler, instilled in me a profound love for the land of my birth and for the language in which I first greeted the world. But they also taught me to respect all of this world's people and cultures. This book is a sad testimony to what happens when that lesson is not put into practice.

KONRAD EISENBICHLER
Victoria College
University of Toronto

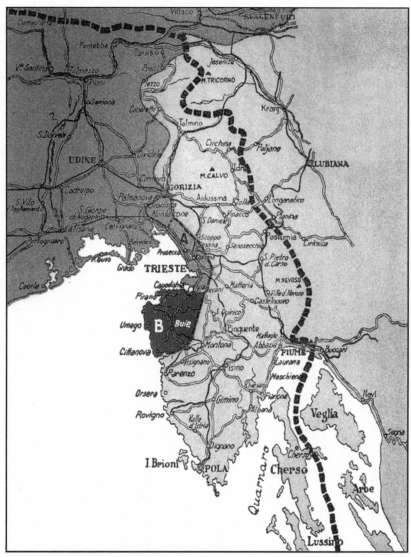

- - - 1924 border
- - - Territory B under temporary Yugoslav administration

Map of Istria, Dalmatia, and Venezia Giulia. From Robert Buranello,
I Giuliano-Dalmati in Canada: Considerazioni ed immagini (New York and
Toronto: Legas, 1995)

A TRAGEDY REVEALED

When ethnicity does not agree with geography, it is ethnicity
that must move.

Benito Mussolini

In 1945 Kardelj and I were sent by Tito into Istria. Our mission
was to use all kinds of pressures to induce all Italians to leave.
And so we did.

Milovan Gilas

1

The Julian Question

A Matter of Gardening

'Sounds like they're nailing down a coffin,' the old man muttered. The men around him wore gloomy expressions and the women were crying silently. A little farther away, the British soldiers were driving long, yellow iron stakes into the ground (figs. 1–2).

A little while later, a young man knelt in front of the first stake and peered down the row.

'If they keep going this way, they'll cut Luca's house in half,' he commented. Then he got up and opened his arms in a forlorn gesture. 'Anyway, my land is all gone.'

A steady, light north wind, the *bora*, was blowing from the Carso Mountains towards the sea. It sent a shiver down the silver branches of the young poplars. Other men went and knelt, as if in prayer, to check the direction indicated by the line of yellow stakes. Then they would get up, swearing under their breath in Triestinian dialect. Nearly all those present spoke Triestinian. A few spoke Slovenian.

The work of the men from the British Royal Engineers Corps was proceeding with exasperating slowness. Every so often, the bleak cadence of the hammer blows was interrupted by the cries of Sergeant MacMuller, a big American who was directing the work with his eye glued to the theodolite, an optical instrument used for topographical measurements.

'Stop!' MacMuller would yell. He would then go and consult with the three officers – an Englishman, an American, and a Yugoslav. Bent over a 1:25,000 map spread out on the grass, they would sink into laborious calculations. All three held the rank of major because, in situations like this, rank equality was a must. Major Milan Grcar, a thickset, blondish Yugoslav, was fussy and litigious. He argued over every decision and often went personally to check the measurements indicated by the theodolite, walking over every step of the contested land. He was ready to raise trouble for a poplar tree or for a foot of land. Major Edward Morris, a rotund, elderly Englishman, was the most accommodating of the three, although he generally sided with Tito's officer. Major William Grover, a young, blond American, nearly a boy, was, in contrast, openly hostile to the Yugoslav.

When the consultation was over, Sergeant MacMuller would turn, bend over his theodolite, and yell his orders to the waiting engineers.

'Ten feet towards Yugoslavia.'

'Four feet towards Italy.'

Ten feet in favour of Yugoslavia, four in favour of Italy ... Those present, nearly all of them local farmers, followed the changes holding their breath. The land the three officers were partitioning was *their* land, *their* livelihood. In the meantime, the American officer was yelling: *'Two inches on your left.'* Two inches to the left ...

Sargeant MacMuller was a veteran of the Second World War and a specialist in this type of border measurement. Two years earlier, at the end of the Korean War, he had traced the border between North and South Korea along the 38th Parallel. 'I hope this border will be less hot than that one,' he would later tell journalists.

It was 7 October 1954. On 5 October, in London, the governments of the United States, Great Britain, Italy, and Yugoslavia had signed the Memorandum of Understanding that put an end to the long-standing and often blood-soaked Julian question, which had been lingering since the end of the Second World War. The memorandum stated that before 26 October, the Free Territory of Trieste, governed up until that point by an Allied military government, would cease to exist and that the two zones into which it had been divided would be assigned to the two bordering countries. Zone A, which ran from Duino to Trieste and was administered by the Allies, would be returned to Italy. Zone B, which ran from Capodistria to Cittanova, had already been assigned to the Yugoslavian civil administration. The memorandum left to Rome and Belgrade the task of settling Zone B's future (see map on p. xv), but there were already clear indications that it would pass to Yugoslavia.

We will later come back to this agreement – later ratified by the Treaty of Osimo in 1975 – which ripped the last patch of Istrian land from Italy. For now, we will limit ourselves to reliving the moments of that last partition.

Zones A and B were separated by the 'Morgan Line,' named after the English officer who drew it in 1945. This rushed and temporary line of demarcation had favoured Yugoslavia, whose delegates at the London Conference had easily been able to obtain corrections and realignments in their favour. In the end, it was decided that the new line, which was to mark the boundary between Italy and Yugoslavia, would begin 'where the 50th parallel meets the coastline' – that is, at the little beach of San Bartolomeo in the municipality of Muggia. From there, it would rise as the crow flies for eight kilometres until it reached Prebenico on the hill of San Michele. 'An insignificant realignment,' the experts had commented, and they were quickly supported by those (including many Italians) who were eager to bring an end to the complicated quarrel between Italy and Yugoslavia, a country that had by then become 'nearly a friend' of Italy. 'Just a matter of gardening,' the newspapers repeated.

In fact, in the context of what had been happening in the region, the partitioning of those few metres of land seemed of consequence to no one. No one, that is, except those directly involved, who followed with anguish the British engineers busy driving yellow stakes into the ground according to Sergeant MacMuller's directions.

Stake after stake, the agony of these people lasted nine days. An adjustment of a mere ten metres, demanded by the obstinate Major Grcar, could decide the fate of a group of houses, a farm, one or more families. In this way, as the relentless yellow line advanced, twenty-seven hamlets belonging to the municipality of Muggia passed to Yugoslavia. Inhabitants who had been sleeping peacefully in their houses, certain of remaining in Italy, hurried to gather their few belongings, load them onto oxcarts, and haul them towards Trieste. Some quickly harvested their corn, others gathered their grapes, still unripened: the last harvests from a land they had owned for generations and that was now being taken from them (figs. 3–4).

The 'human cases' that remained unsolved, despite Major Grover's good intentions, were in the hundreds. A little distance from the mouth of San Bartolomeo Creek stood the chalet Caravella belonging to the Triestinian Umberto Greatti, who had gone deep into debt to build it. They ignored his protests and took it from him. The Caravella had been opened in March 1953. It was only eighteen months old.

As the young man who had knelt and studied the direction of the yellow stakes had foretold, Luca Eller's house was cut in two: kitchen and bedrooms in Italy, living room and storehouse in Yugoslavia. From the Pecchiar family, who hailed from the Rabuiese area on the road between Trieste and Skofije (Scoffie), they took only the barnyard and chicken coop. In short, they were repeating the same absurd partitions that had been carried out years before in the area of Gorizia, where even a cemetery had been casually cut in two.

In the town of Crevatini, assigned after a long squabble to Yugoslavia, all the inhabitants without exception chose the painful road of exile. One of them, the bricklayer Luigi Crevatini, had moved to Fiume before the war. When the war was about to end, he had come back to Capodistria; then in 1945, to flee the *Titini* (as Tito's forces were called), he had returned to his birthplace, still in Zone A. He was sure he was finally safe, but instead he was again forced to pack his bags. 'But this time,' he protested, 'I'm going as far away as possible. Perhaps to Sicily.' For his part, the road tender Mario Borrini, a native of Massa Carrara in Tuscany, was happy with the advancing border. And not only because his house was left in Italy, but also because, as he explained: 'Some time ago the length of road assigned to my care reached all the way to Capodistria, then they took away the section between Capodistria and Albaro Vescovà. Now I will have yet another kilometre of road less to tend.'

The Samec family from Belpoggio was also miraculously spared. According to Major Grcar, their house, one of a group of seven, should have passed to Yugoslavia. They had already gathered their belongings and were ready to seek refuge in Muggia when, thanks to Major Grover, the border commission realized it had made an error of twenty metres. The Samecs returned home, still in Italy.

Major Grover did all he could to resolve in the kindest possible way the most painful 'human cases' created by that inexorable line, which sliced the land like a scalpel cutting living flesh. But the obstinate Major Grcar would not let go. Often he would go consult with a group of his people, who were standing off to the side: men in uniform, each with a red star on his service cap, surrounding a terse and distant man in civilian clothes, the political commissar. Then he would return, more obstinate than before.

Those who stood to be evicted stayed around their houses until the last moment in the hope that the advancing stakes would change course. Heart-breaking scenes followed. Few families, not all of them Slovenian, accepted their fate willingly. Most defended their property until the bitter end, with the men cursing and the women crying. An old farmer, Giovanni Bort, hurled to the ground the last basket of unripened grapes he had gathered, then angrily threw his hat against the Yugoslavian officer: 'I'll have my house in Zone A and my farm in Zone B,' he yelled. 'History will remember these mistakes!' A farmer from Cerei confronted the commission and shouted: 'You have stolen my destiny.' Before going away, Ignazio Babich, who lived in Bosini, loaded onto his cart the bricks he would have used to build his chicken coop: 'I don't want them to build it for themselves with my materials,' he explained. The village of Chiampre was cut precisely in half. Italy was left with the church, the school, and a few houses. Major Grcar was seen to smile when on one of the houses assigned to Yugoslavia he read the sign 'People's House Alma Vivoda': it was the local headquarters of the Communist Party. One last, bitter curiosity: as had been the case before, first in Pola and then in the area of Gorizia, the refugees left the front doors of their houses wide open. What was the point of locking them, anyway ...

Overall, 'Operation Gardening' had cost Italy twenty-seven hamlets with 1,340 families – a total of 3,855 people. Already by the end of that week, 2,941 of them had 'opted for freedom,' knowing full well that Italy would not welcome them with open arms. They were the last small change from a cheque for the Second World War that the region of Venezia Giulia was paying on behalf of all Italians.

On the evening of 25 October 1954, while the Italian Bersaglieri[1] were gathering at Duino on their way to Trieste, the Yugoslavian troops formed a bridgehead along the new border. Behind them, trucks filled with the settlers who would be taking over the abandoned houses were on their way. In the darkness, one could hear the Communist anthem, 'Bandiera rossa' being sung a little sleepily in Italian.

The following day, the *Giornale di Trieste*, alluding to the blatant British favouritism on behalf of Yugoslavia, published a revealing cartoon. It showed Marshal Tito jumping gleefully over the old 'Morgan Line,' watched by two friendly 'gentlemen' in top hats and coat-tails. One of them was saying: 'One must admit that Tito did all he could to come over to our side.'

Some time later, the Istrian writer Pier Antonio Quarantotti Gambini, a refugee living in Trieste, recalling the celebrations marking the return

---

1 Founded in 1836 as an elite corps of highly mobile soldiers, the Bersaglieri are easily identifiable by their rakish plumed helmets, their brisk, on-the-double march, and the spirited trumpet fanfare that accompanies them. From the very beginning, they have embodied the best and most genuine in the Italian spirit and have won many military honours in many a conflict (translator's note).

of the city to Italy, wrote in his diary: 'I don't know with what feelings the hundreds of thousands of Triestinians who sang the praises of Italy and its soldiers gathered in their houses on the evening of the 26th. I, for one, when I opened my desk that evening, felt a shiver down my spine as I saw there, in front of me, some red-white-and-green flyers that said: *Triestinians, do you remember your forty days under the Titini? We have been living these days for a year, now. Help us!* Leaflets disseminated by Istrians in the spring of 1946.'

Trieste did not help the Istrians, and neither did Rome. But that is a story which must be told from the beginning.

The Mosaic Gone Mad

In border regions not marked out by nature (that is, by rivers, seas, mountain ranges), even when two ethnic groups do not tend to mix, it has always been difficult to draw boundaries that satisfy both groups. Over the years, in fact, human migrations, not to mention land grabs arising from long-ago conflicts, result in a mosaic gone mad, one in which it is nearly always impossible to discern any boundaries. And in which, during moments of crisis, each side can easily find justifications for attacking the other. 'In political geography,' wrote Ambrose Bierce in his caustic *The Unabridged Devil's Dictionary*, 'the border is that imaginary line between two nations that separates the imagined rights of one people from those of the other.' The supreme example of all this is ex-Yugoslavia, a multinational country that was held together for a time by centralist forces. Once those forces weakened, the ethnic groups that were part of that state went back to fighting one another, fully convinced that God and history were on their side.

For some years, we have watched with horror the blood-soaked dissolution of Yugoslavia, which was born in 1918 around the conference tables of Versailles and strengthened around those of Paris and London after the Second World War. All the nationalities that constituted it are now in turmoil: Croatians, Slovenians, Serbians, Bosnians, Montenegrins, Kosovars ... all except one: the Italians, with their deep historical roots in Venezia Giulia, in Istria, and in Dalmatia. Why? The explanation is dramatically simple: in those regions where one still finds Roman remains, lions of St Mark, and lictorian fasces, there are no more Italians. The few who still live there are the descendants of those who, after the Second World War, chose to become Yugoslav; the rest ended up by the thousands in the *foibe*, the mountain crevasses of the

Carso, or were forced in the hundreds of thousands into exile. Today, the survivors of this ethnic cleansing are scattered throughout Italy and the world. Theirs is a diaspora for which Italy has shown itself to be downright ungrateful and even hypocritical.

Yet the uprooting of the Italian people of the Julian regions along the eastern Adriatic cannot, of course, change the history that led up to it. As everyone knows, the Italian presence in those regions is ancient. First the Romans and then the Venetians brought their civilization there, and this is an irrefutable fact. This is not to deny that over the centuries, constant human migrations created that mosaic gone mad we noted earlier. Let us therefore set aside the vanities of primogeniture along with the statistics drawn from various censuses, which in any case always prove to be deceptive and contradictory. Let us consider, instead, recent history.

Towards the end of the nineteenth century, when these regions were still part of the Hapsburg Empire, Italians were the majority in the cities but nearly absent in the countryside ('Italian islands in a Slavic sea,' a Croatian nationalist would call them). To dampen the growing Italian nationalist movement fed by the winds of the Risorgimento blowing in from the peninsula, the Austrian government sought in every way to encourage an influx of Slavic populations into the coastal region and to block the immigration of the *regnicoli* – that is, Italians from the kingdom (*regno*) of Italy.

By the beginning of the twentieth century, thanks to an economic boom, Trieste had become, after Vienna, Prague, and Budapest, the empire's fourth-largest city (230,000 people). As a result of this boom, Trieste, which at one time had been completely Italian, within a few decades was only by majority Italian (25 per cent were now Slavic, 5 per cent German). According to the Triestinian historian Glauco Arneri, had the First World War not erupted, Italians would have become a minority in Trieste because the rate of Slavic migration to the city would have quickly raised its population beyond half a million.

The predominantly Slavic Catholic priests were fervent supporters of the Hapsburg government and actively favoured this process. In those years, Catholic Austria stood against lay Italy, which had not only destroyed the Papal States but also confined the Pope to the Vatican. From the pulpits of country churches, priests cast the landowners (nearly always Italian) as Masons, unbelievers, or Jews, in contrast to the humble farmers (always Slavic), whom they always presented as devout Catholics and as faithful subjects of the emperor. In the same way that nationality would later be tied to politics (Italians = Fascists, Slavs = Communists), at that time nationality was tied to religion (Slavs = filo-Austrian Catholics, Italians = irredentist atheists).

So it can be stated that on the whole, Catholic priests were fomenting Slavic nationalism in the countryside. And these priests were numerous as well as influential. The historian Paola Romano notes that at the beginning of the twentieth century, 190 of the 290 priests in the diocese of Trieste were Slavs, and that in Istria the liturgy was even celebrated in the local language, Schiavetto.

This idiom, which prevailed in the countryside, leads us into a digression that will certainly help us understand the relationship between the Italian and Slavic elements of the population, more so than many sociological studies. Already at the time of the Most Serene Republic of Venice, the non-Venetian inhabitants of the eastern Adriatic seaboard were called, in a derogatory way, Schiavi (later transformed into Slavi). The Doge's Dalmatian guards were the Schiavoni, and Slavonia was the land of the Schiavi and Schiavetto was their dialect, which was rich in Venetian words that had been Slavicized.

Beginning in the middle of the nineteenth century, when a gale of revolution aroused the nationalism that had been slumbering in the various regions of the Hapsburg Empire, new cultural elites – Croatian, Serbian, Slovenian – appeared on the scene. More than against Austria, they directed their attacks against the Italians, who in those regions were the bourgeoisie. The first to ignite the powder keg were the Croatians, who advanced their cause with ferocity, so much so that the Dalmatian writer Niccolò Tommaseo (1802–74) remarked that 'the Croatians use stones like commas and guns like exclamation marks.' They demanded that the Austrian government annex Dalmatia, whose cities had been made wealthy by Italian entrepreneurs and industry. The Slovenians, for their part, yearned to expand into Venezia Giulia, drawn by the flourishing city of Trieste, where there were already more Slovenians than in Ljubljana. Meanwhile, the Serbians, obsessed by the myth of a Greater Serbia, pursued the dream of becoming 'the Piedmont of the Balkans' and extending their hegemony over all the southern Slavic states.

Although divided by deep ancestral hatreds that are still digging deep trenches between their various nationalities, these Slavic populations had found a bond – the inferiority complex they shared vis-à-vis the Italians, a non-Slavic people whom they saw as intruders.

The 'Crippled Victory'

When the First World War erupted on 28 July 1914, the antagonism between Italians and Slavs within the Hapsburg Empire reached a flashpoint. As a result of recent migrations, the Slavs had become an important electoral force (in Venezia Giulia alone, about 350,000 Italians squared off against some 470,000 Slavs). Italians now found themselves in a delicate situation. They were now almost foreigners in their native land.

In Italy's political circles, the Austro-Italian conflict had given rise to two contradictory responses among interventionists. Some Italians, the futurists and nationalist firebrands, such as Gabriele D'Annunzio and Benito Mussolini, spoke of a 'beautiful war, the only cleanser of the world,' and expressed through their interventionist ideals a strong imperialist will. And some, democratic leftists such as Gaetano Salvemini, Pietro Nenni, and Antonio Gramsci, saw the war as the natural outgrowth of the national unification process that had begun with the Risorgimento.

The Julian, Istrian, and Dalmatian irredentists obviously belonged to the second group. They saw the conflict as the only possible means to reunite with the motherland. Their contribution to the Italian military effort was significant: more than 2,000 Julians deserted the Austrian army and risked the gallows in order to don the grey-green uniform of the Italians. They earned 11 gold medals, 183 silver, and 145 bronze. They suffered 302 dead and nearly 500 wounded. Four of them, captured in Italian uniform and charged with treason, ended their lives on the gallows. Their names have been written on the scroll of Italian war heroes: Nazario Sauro from Capodistria, Cesare Battisti from Trento, Francesco Rismondo from Spalato, and Fabio Filzi from Pisino.

After the Italian victory in 1918 – a victory that D'Annunzio would refer to as 'crippled' precisely because of the controversies surrounding the fate of the Istrian and Dalmatian territories – Italian and Slavic nationalisms began to clash once again. Even though the Slavs had fought loyally for Austro-Hungary, their leaders were able to insert themselves into the diplomatic game. The creation of the Yugoslav state as a federation of southern Slavic countries reopened complex and heated border questions. For example, France and England did not favour Italian expansion into the ex-Hapsburg provinces, even though the Italians had helped them win the war, and were open to Yugoslavian demands that the new border extend to the Tagliamento River; this border would have brought the city of Udine into Yugoslavian territory. President Woodrow Wilson of the United States further complicated matters when – perhaps accustomed to drawing boundaries across empty lands or lands without history (such as those of the United States) – he recommended that the new border be laid out 'along clearly visible national lines.' This was a foretaste of the American principle of the right of self-determination, which during the post-1945 era would lead to complex international disputes.

In the months that followed, the disagreements among the winning powers intensified. The 'Wilson Line,' which assigned eastern Istria and Dalmatia to Yugoslavia, had enraged the Italian public. In teary-eyed protest, the Italian prime minister, Vittorio Emanuele Orlando, had abandoned the Paris Peace Conference. The poet–soldier Gabriele D'Annunzio, for his part, led a small armed force of volunteers to occupy the city of Fiume; on 8 September 1920, he established the Regency of the Carnaro, a 'free state' that would be destroyed in the 'Bloody Christmas' of 1920, in a fratricidal encounter between the Fiumani legionnaires and regular units of the Italian Royal Army led by General Enrico Caviglia.

The problem of the border with Yugoslavia was partially resolved by the Treaty of Rapallo of 12 November 1920. It declared Fiume a 'free city' and assigned to Italy all of Istria as well as the Dalmatian city of Zara and the Adriatic islands of Cherso, Lussino, Lagosta, and Pelagosa. The Belgrade government, however, did not want to ratify the treaty; it saw that 'agreement' as an ultimatum and refused to present it to its Parliament. Only in 1927, with the Pacts of Rome signed by the Italian Prime Minister Benito Mussolini and his Yugoslavian counterpart Nikola Pašić, was the treaty ratified by Yugoslavia. The problem of Fiume was resolved by the awarding of that city to Italy and Porto Barros to Yugoslavia.

Having acquired Fiume, Pola, and Zara, Italy had finally reached the eastern borders imagined by the theorists of the Risorgimento. But the acquisition of lands that had historically been Italian did not mean that all their inhabitants were happy to become Italian.

Promises Not Kept

In defence of the Treaty of Rapallo and in response to the Socialists, who were demanding guarantees for the Slavic minority, the Italian foreign minister, Carlo Sforza, declared to the Chamber of Deputies: 'We will guarantee to these citizens freedom of language and culture. This is a point of honour for us. It is also wise politics.'

Sacred words, but also the vain promises of a liberal Italy about to vanish. In truth, even under the final pre-Fascist governments, in the 'redeemed' provinces Italian nationalism had begun to reveal its aggressive face: it was now moving towards the removal or the falsification of centuries of history it considered shameful, even to the point of demolishing the vestiges of that history. For example, in 1919 in Trieste, the monument of the city's *Dedication* to the Hapsburgs was destroyed overnight. In 1920, the statue of Maximilian of Austria, the Emperor of Mexico executed by firing squad at Queretaro in 1867, was removed. The following year, the statue of Empress Elisabeth, the wildly popular 'Sissi.'[2] was also removed; it would not be restored to its place until 1997.

As the peace treaty took hold, an ethnic transformation began in the new provinces as a result of the exodus of those who rejected Italian citizenship. The first to leave had been the Austrian bourgeoisie and the bureaucrats of the old imperial administration. They were soon followed by the more recent Slavic bourgeoisie, called back by the opportunities the new Yugoslavia offered them. The Croatian and Slovenian farmers felt an old and strong attachment to their land, and preferred to remain. However, it should be pointed out that this exodus was a result not of political pressure, but rather of economic crisis. Once the euphoria of victory had subsided, the entire 'redeemed' region found itself having to adapt to new realities, which in many ways were not positive. Trieste in particular was suffering in this new era. Its port, once prosperous because it was the Hapsburg Empire's major seaport, now faced competition from the many other harbours in Italy. This, and inflation and the flight of foreign capital, impoverished many inhabitants of the city. The beautiful, rich, and cosmopolitan city, whose charms had attracted artists and visitors from all over Europe, quickly decayed into a nondescript Italian provincial town.

In the meantime, thousands of families from southern Italy had moved north to fill, however inadequately, the void created by the voluntary exodus of Austrians and Slavs. After the United States closed its borders to immigration, these families sought a better life in these new Italian territories.

---

2 Empress of Austria and Queen of Hungary, the immensely popular Elisabeth, beloved wife of Emperor Franz Joseph, was assassinated in 1898 by an anarchist (translator's note).

The ethnic transformation of the Julian population was already obvious in the election of 15 May 1921, when Slavs won only five out of the fifteen seats in Venezia Giulia. A later census revealed that Italians now constituted 58 per cent of the population and Slavs 39 per cent.

But censuses and elections are not enough to draw an accurate picture of the situation. As had happened under the Hapsburgs, both could be manipulated and exploited. We know, for example, that especially in industrial centres, even the Slavic workers voted for Italian political parties of the Left. And in the censuses, many Julians declared themselves Italian one day, Slavic the next, according to the benefits thereby accorded them.

In 1922, with the victory of Fascism and the subsequent persecution of parties of the Left, the picture became much more complex. The 'frontier Fascists' soon revealed themselves to be much more aggressive than their urban counterparts, both because of their bullying instincts and because they were often provoked by Croatian and Slovenian nationalists, who were animated by similar nationalist sentiments. Incidents and clashes were numerous. Not even the iron fist of the regime was able to normalize the situation. Many Slavs who were determined not to be Italianized embraced the Communist doctrine, even though they themselves were not Communists, for the simple reason that at that moment in time the internationalist doctrine preached by Lenin provided a home for their frustrated nationalism. This contradiction would show its explosive consequences during the Second World War.

Mussolini's government presented two distinct faces to Venezia Giulia. On the economic side, it began important reclamation projects that turned malarial swamps into flourishing fields; it also undertook large-scale public works projects that transformed the region economically by eliminating unemployment and encouraging an influx of workers from southern Italy. New factories, aqueducts, power stations, shipyards, mines, roads, and railways all greatly improved the quality of life of the people, and did so without discrimination. On the political side, however, the situation was different.

'When ethnicity does not agree with geography,' Mussolini had declared before dealing with the Adriatic problem, 'it is ethnicity that must move.' These brutal but clear words summarized his intentions. On 7 November 1922, only a few days after becoming prime minister, he signed a decree that suppressed the commissariats for the new provinces, which he had accused of being too soft on Slavs. He then created the provinces of Trieste and Pola and placed them in the hands of prefects allied with the regime. He also incorporated the entire region of Gorizia into the province of Udine 'to drown its numerous Slavs in an ocean of Friulians.' In 1923, with the school reforms of Giovanni Gentile, all Slavic schools were closed, and in Italian schools the study of the Italian language was imposed as *fundamental and exclusive*. Slavic teachers were fired on various pretexts; Slavic priests were forbidden to teach their language or even to use it (or Schiavetto) in their liturgical celebrations. All Slavic periodicals in the region were suppressed, and the use of the Slavic language in public offices or courts was banned.

In 1926, after the Italian legislature reintroduced the death penalty, the Special Tribunal for the Defence of the State – an instrument created by the regime specifically to block any form of political opposition – was set up. Between 1926 and 1943, the Trieste Tribunal pronounced two hundred sentences against Slovenian and Croatian nationalists, handing out more than two thousand years of jail time or internal exile, as well ten death sentences, which were duly carried out.

Forbidden Surnames

The campaign to Italianize Venezia Giulia built up steam. After the official use of Italian was imposed, the use of Slavic languages even in conversation became dangerous. Signs reading 'Italian spoken here' appeared in stores and public venues. Slavic choirs were forbidden to sing their songs at feasts. This campaign reached its height in 1927, when the government imposed Italianization of place names and family names. This stage turned out to be rather complicated and severely taxed those charged with its implementation. Often, for place names, there already existed a word in both languages (Pola = Pula, Fiume = Rijeka, Parenzo = Porek, Capodistria = Koper, and so on). With Slavic family names, the process was more difficult; these had to be transformed into Italian names. This was sometimes done by deleting the classic ending in 'ch' or 'ć'; but other times the exercise was more arbitrary. As an example, here is part of the directive from the prefect of Pola to the registry offices of the municipalities and to the school boards: 'In order to remove the mangling of surnames perpetrated in the last few decades by Slavic petty politicians, I decree that the surnames of the inhabitants of this municipality be written as indicated below.' There follows a long list of Slavic surnames rendered into Italian: Andretich = Andretti, Burich = Bubbi, Pulich = Pulli, Volcić = Volci, Vidalich = Vidali, and so on. Among the victims of this paradoxical cleansing were some very illustrious family names whose members subsequently chose to retain the new Italian version, such as Senator for Life Leo Valiani, whose name as a young student in Fiume in 1927 was Leo Weiczen. One must add, however, that many influential families, such as Cosulich, Suvić, Bisiach, and Illić, were allowed to retain their original surnames without any problem.

Naturally, this intolerant, discriminatory, and in some ways racist politic adopted by Rome provoked a reaction from the Slavs, a reaction that soon enough turned violent. In those areas where the Slavic presence was especially strong, there arose secret societies that occasionally organized assaults and outright guerrilla actions. These societies had links with and were assisted by various Slavic and Croatian nationalist groups that were already operating clandestinely in Yugoslavia. The Slavic irredentists were not, however, unified in their activities: deep-seated hatreds and resentments divided them along ethnic lines, as they still do. These divisions naturally facilitated the work of the Italian police, who, however, failed to wipe out the secret organizations in spite of the many arrests, deportations, and executions. In the end, with the help of the Italian Communist Party, which was already well represented in the region by clandestine cells, the various Slavic groups formed a common front, which during the Second World War developed into the Yugoslav Resistance Movement.

Blow and Counter-Blow between Rome and Belgrade

In the interwar years, diplomatic relations between Italy and Yugoslavia were characterized by a constant and lively antagonism in which moments of calm alternated with moments of barely suppressed hostility. The main cause of friction was the problem of the minorities: the Slavic one in Italy and the Italian one in Dalmatia. The Belgrade government was certainly no more gentle in its dealings with its Italian-speaking citizens than the Italian government was towards its Slavic minority. In fact, in some cases the anti-Slavic measures implemented in Venezia Giulia were simply responses to similar measures implemented in Dalmatia. For example, the suppression of the teaching of Slavic languages in Julian schools was a reaction against an analogous decree for Dalmatian schools issued by Yugoslav authorities.

Beyond this, however, there were other reasons why relations between the two countries remained extremely tense. In those years, Italy openly aspired to extend its influence over the entire Balkan Peninsula, which in part meant fostering the growth of those movements which had taken Italian Fascism as their model. Italy's alliance with Hungary, ruled by the dictator Admiral Horthy, the marriage of Princess Giovanna di Savoia to King Boris of Bulgaria, and the financial support extended to the Iron Guards of Codreanu and Antonescu in Romania, not to mention the 'protectorate' status granted to Albania, were all part of Mussolini's ambitious project of extending Italian influence over the region.

The only country to resist Rome's enticement was the newly created Yugoslavia. As an extremely young state, its borders drawn up at a conference table by France and England after the First World War, the 'Kingdom of the Serbians, Croatians, and Slovenians' (as it was officially styled so as not to ruffle the sensibilities of its three major ethnic groups) owed its existence to an Anglo-French project to restrict Italy's expansionist designs. Its creation was the result of complex negotiations and not-always-logical compromises. The end result was a mosaic-state that gathered under the crown of the King of Serbia, Alexander I Karagjergjević, various regions with different cultures and languages pulled from the ruins of the Hapsburg and the Ottoman empires. Yugoslavia's twelve million people belonged to groups that were hostile to one another (Serbians, Croatians, Slovenians, Bosnians, Macedonians, Montenegrins, Dalmatians, Morlacchi, Kosovars, not to mention the Italian, Austrian, and Magyar minorities). Nor were these people united by a common religion, for some were Catholic, others Orthodox, and others Moslem.

The internal situation of Yugoslavia was thus very different from that of other Balkan nations: the jealousies among Serbians, Slovenians, and Croatians, and the hopes for independence held by all the nationalities that comprised it, made this a very fragile state and one especially sensitive to external pressures. Mussolini was the first to seek to profit from this.

'All Serbians and Everywhere'

Serbians and Croatians have always been divided by an ancestral hatred that has literally shed rivers of blood. Only Marshal Tito (who was Croatian, but who hid his origins) was able to make them live together for a few decades, but only thanks to an iron fist. Once Tito was gone, everything went back to what it was before. King Alexander I, who was Serbian and did not hide it, was unable to use an iron fist against his Croatian subjects; they had accepted him with reluctance, and they continued to dream of an independent Croatian state. As a result, even though the central government had granted them extensive autonomy, the Croatians found almost unbearable the intrusiveness and arrogance of the Serbian bureaucrats who had taken control of the kingdom's administration. Friction was constant. Croatia teemed with secret societies that adhered to a famous slogan of the time: 'God in heaven, only Croatians in our Motherland, and only Croatians to rule in Croatia!' For their part, the Serbians had a slogan of their own in which one can already hear the warning signs of the ethnic cleansing that would make a bloodbath of Yugoslavia: 'The Serbian sky is blue. In heaven a Serbian God sits on the throne, with Serbian angels sitting beside him who honour their Serbian God. Serbians all of them and everywhere!' Words heavy as stones, especially since everyone on both sides was determined to abide by them.

The Assassination of King Alexander I

For the two belligerent ethnic groups, cohabitation was not a long-term arrangement. After a series of disagreements, tragedy struck in 1928, when Serbian and Croatian deputies engaged in a shoot-out in Parliament that left three Croatian parliamentarians dead on the floor of the House and another ten wounded. After this episode, the Serbian faction forced the king to abolish Parliament, and the army – entirely Serbian – seized power.

Naturally, the Croatians' answer was not long in coming. The Croatians established a terrorist organization with Fascist learnings to fight for an independent Croatia, whose boundaries would extend beyond Trieste to the Isonzo and Tagliamento rivers. The leader of this movement, called the Ustachi, was an ex-schoolteacher named Ante Pavelić, an unscrupulous fanatic who did not hesitate to accept the self-interested help of Mussolini. Setting aside for the moment his ambitions for Venezia Giulia, Pavelić took good advantage of Italian protection.

Mussolini had his own reasons for encouraging Yugoslavia to tear itself apart. That country's government, meanwhile, had drawn close to France. Mussolini was already supporting the Macedonian nationalists by providing them with 44 million lire. With Pavelić (who, to ingratiate himself with his protector, had assumed the title of 'Poglavnik,' the Croatian equivalent of 'Duce'), Mussolini was even more generous. Besides extending financial assistance, he allowed the Ustachi to set up refugee camps in Italy: at Borgotaro sulla Cisa, at San

Demetrio in the province of L'Aquila, and in a wooded area outside Arezzo. Pavelić, with his wife and three children, set himself up in Bologna. Other Ustachi bases were later established in Germany and Hungary.

In those years, many terrorist attacks were launched from the Italian camps, where the Ustachi were trained in the techniques of terrorism. The group's most spectacular success was the double-assassination, in Marseille in 1934, of King Alexander I, who had just arrived on a state visit to France, and the French foreign minister, Jean-Louis Barthou, who had come to greet him.

This attack filled Europe with horror. Strong accusations were immediately levelled at Mussolini, whom Belgrade did not hesitate to finger as the commissioner. There is, however, no evidence of Italian complicity in that particular act, nor are there any obvious reasons why Italy would have approved or supported it. According to the historian Renzo De Felice, it is much more plausible that there was some German or Hungarian involvement, for both these governments were in close contact with the Ustachi. That said, the assassins had come from Italy, and in Rome, the Fascist secret police, the OVRA, had even created a 'Croatia Office' charged with bankrolling the terrorists' activities. Pavelić was arrested in Bologna, but he was never handed over to the Yugoslavs, who had condemned him in absentia to death and were now asking for his extradition.

Contrary to the hopes of the Croatian terrorists, Alexander's assassination did not lead to the collapse of the Yugoslav state. It merely aggravated the already strained relations between Belgrade and Rome and favoured the Serbian faction. The king's premature death created an institutional void, since the young heir, who would become Peter II, had not yet reached the age of majority. The Serbian army took advantage of this situation to set up a Regency Council under the direction of Prince Paul, the deceased king's brother. The new government imposed a right-wing dictatorship on the country and immediately banned the Communist Party; however, it resisted both the enticements and the threats of Fascist Italy and Nazi Germany, both of which were attempting to draw Yugoslavia into their orbit. The Regent Paul sought, instead, to regain the trust of the Western powers by making a show of pro-British sentiments, and he did not hesitate to side with England and France when, on the occasion of the Italian invasion of Ethiopia, the League of Nations, which those two countries controlled, imposed economic sanctions against Italy.

Belgrade Rescinds the Triple Alliance

When the Second World War erupted after the German invasion of Poland in September 1939, the Balkan peninsula was within the Italo-German sphere of influence, except for neutral Yugoslavia (and for Greece, traditionally tied to England). Some time before this, Italy had taken possession of Albania following a rapid *coup de main*. Hungary, Romania, and Bulgaria, long allied with Berlin, were about to sign the Triple Alliance, which would draw them definitely into the conflict. The Alliance pact, signed in September 1939 by the three Axis powers (Germany, Italy, and Japan), obliged the signatories to uphold rigorously all of its clauses, including the one relating to freedom of access for Axis troops. The pact's objectives were crystal clear in the first two clauses:

> *Clause One*: Japan recognizes and respects the leadership of Germany and Italy in the creation of a New Order in Europe.
> *Clause Two*: Germany and Italy recognize and respect the leadership of Japan in the creation of a New Order in the Great Asian East.

It was also clear that any third party that signed the pact would be required to accept meekly the rank of satellite country to the Axis. Through enticements and threats, Berlin's emissaries easily persuaded the governments of Budapest, Bucharest, and Sofia to accept the *diktat*. Only Belgrade was obstinately determined to remain neutral.

In Rome and Berlin throughout the first year of the war, no one doubted the pro-British sympathies of the Regent, Prince Paul. Even so, the Axis powers left the Yugoslav government free to tend to its internal conflicts, which were growing more complicated every day. At this time, the Balkans were of secondary importance in Hitler's war strategy. The Führer still shared Bismarck's opinion that 'the Balkans are not worth the bones of a single Pomeranian grenadier' and considered that region to be useful only as a food source and, above all, for the Romanian oilfields, the only energy source available to the Reich. Only later, once the German High Command began in absolute secrecy to prepare Operation Barbarossa against the Soviet Union, would it become indispensable for Berlin to cover its back and ensure that it controlled the entire region.

By the autumn of 1940, after the Italians impulsively invaded Greece, the situation in the Balkans had deteriorated. Mussolini's rash act had very much irritated Hitler and surprised international observers. That war made no sense: Greece was no threat on the Mediterranean chessboard; furthermore, it was already governed by a quasi-fascist regime. Mussolini had been advised by his staff to invade it in the hope of gaining an easy victory that would strengthen the public's approval of his government, which was weakening as a result of military setbacks on other fronts. His foreign minister, Galeazzo Ciano, had been the main proponent of the plan. He had assured the Duce that his only worry was to have 'enough fuel to arrive in twenty-four hours to Salonika [Thessaloniki].' But everything went contrary to expectations: the blitz failed, and the Greeks defended themselves heroically – in their counteroffensive, they even advanced into Albanian territory. Eventually, the retreating Italians were obliged to wait for the Germans to arrive and rescue them from their fix.

By February 1941, the Wehrmacht was massing divisions in Hungary, Romania, and Bulgaria, and Belgrade was suffering through long, anxious days. The Yugoslavs did not know that the troops being concentrated next door were destined for Operation Barbarossa, so they feared that their time to face Germany was drawing near. In those frenzied days, intrigues and plots abounded; Prince Paul was negotiating secretly with German and British envoys without resolving the impasse over signing the Triple Alliance. The Germans brutally threatened to put Yugoslavia to fire and sword if it did not adhere to the *diktat*, while the British encouraged him to resist it and were lavish with promises, which Tito would later collect on, much to the embarrassment of the British government (some of these promises concerned Venezia Giulia, as would later be revealed).

After a series of dramatic clashes with Berlin's envoys and with Hitler himself, in the end Prince Paul gave up. On 25 March 1941, during a heavily publicized meeting in Vienna with the Führer, he signed the Triple Alliance. The event was broadcast live on radio across Europe, and some clauses especially favourable to Yugoslavia that had been added to the document's original text were highlighted. One of these said that the Axis powers would 'at every moment respect the sovereignty and territorial integrity of Yugoslavia.' Another promised that 'Yugoslavia will not be involved in this war and will not be asked to permit the passage of Axis troops over its territory.'

The event was greeted with enthusiasm in Croatia, but was harshly condemned in Serbia in spite of the enticing concessions. With the stubbornness and proud recklessness that have always characterized them, the Serbians rebelled against the Nazis. In the end, the Regency Council repudiated Prince Paul (who on his return was deposed and arrested), and the army sided with the rebels. The following day, after Prime Minister Dušan Simović officially denounced the Triple Alliance, popular enthusiasm overflowed everywhere. Immediately, as if by magic, the windows of Belgrade were festooned with French and British flags. Crowds danced in the streets, and the Serbian national anthem could be heard everywhere: 'Better war, better death than slavery ...'

On 28 March, a solemn ceremony was held in the Orthodox cathedral in Belgrade. The church soon filled with an excited crowd calling loudly for the new king, Peter II. The Crown Prince was still six months shy of eighteen and was being confined to the palace by his tutors. He managed, nonetheless, to escape their surveillance, climb down a drain pipe to the street, and reach the church. Thanks to a special decree immediately approved by the government, the young prince was proclaimed king six months before his time. His coronation was triumphal and moving.

The events in Belgrade made quite an impression internationally. For the first time, a small country had dared resist the Nazis' arrogance. In London, Winston Churchill swore eternal gratitude to the heroic Yugoslavs. In the United States, the *New York Times* described the *coup d'état* in Belgrade as 'lightning that lights up the darkness.'

In Berlin there was, naturally, an equal but opposite reaction. Hitler flew into 'one of the most violent rages in all his life.' He immediately convened his military commanders and, pounding the conference table with his fists, ordered them to destroy Yugoslavia 'militarily and politically, without any diplomatic overtures, without any ultimatum, and without waiting for any declaration of loyalty from the new government.' They were to prepare without delay a plan for the invasion of Yugoslavia and of Greece as well. Having been blindsided, Hitler made his intentions crystal clear: he would erase Yugoslavia from the map and distribute its territories among the neighbouring countries, which had been yearning for some time to divide it among themselves. He then dictated a long telegram to Mussolini in which he invited the Duce to claw into Yugoslavia himself.

Many German generals spent that night awake. By four in the morning, General Alfred Jodl, head of operations for the Wehrmacht, was able to give General Enno von Rintelen, liaison officer between the German High Command and its Italian counterpart, instructions for the Italians that would allow the two allies to proceed 'with extreme speed' in coordinating German operations with those of Italians in Greece. The Germans did not tell the Italians the real reason for this urgency, which was, that they were worried the Yugoslav army might retreat from the German invasion by crossing the Albanian border, thus overtaking the Italian troops fighting on the Greek front.

Air Blitz against Belgrade

'Operation Punishment,' as it was called in code, began at dawn on 6 April 1941 with a violent air attack on Belgrade. For twenty-four solid hours, swarms of Stuka bombers pounded the helpless city, almost flattening it. German divisions gathered at the borders, waiting for the order to occupy the country. The German High Command was certain that the relentless air assault would compel the government to sue for peace immediately. But the Yugoslavs, true to their nature, stubbornly resisted the avalanche of fire.

By dawn on 9 April 1941, it was clear that the Yugoslav government had no intention of surrendering, so the great land invasion began along the entire border. German armoured divisions in Austria, Hungary, Romania, and Bulgaria crossed the border and headed directly for Belgrade. At the same time, the Hungarians took back without resistance their ancient territories, while the Italian Second Army under General Vittorio Ambrosio, moving out from Venezia Giulia, quickly conquered Ljubljana and Karlovac, and then proceeded along the Dalmatian coast to Ragusa (Dubrovnik). There, it joined up with the Italian troops returning from Albania. Within four days, the Yugoslav army no longer existed. A day before that, the young Peter II and his government had fled to Greece; from there, under British protection, they would be lifted to Palestine.

The blitz on Yugoslavia was followed a few days later by a blitz on Greece. Without catching their breath, the Germans fell on that ancient country, where the Italians had been bogged down for months. By 28 April 1941, the Swastika and the Italian flag were flying atop the Parthenon. The Balkan campaign was over: the Axis forces now dominated Europe from the Baltic to the Aegean.

This strategic diversion, which Yugoslav obstinacy and Greek resistance had imposed on Hitler, would have serious repercussions for the Axis. First, the Balkan campaign delayed the start of Operation Barbarossa by four weeks, with grave consequences for the Germans. Second, in their rush to reach Greece, the Germans had not bothered to disarm the Yugoslavs, considering their army destroyed. But the

Yugoslavs would use the weapons they still had to bring into being a partisan struggle unique in Europe.

Dividing Up the Cake

With Yugoslavia wiped off the map, cartographers traced a new series of lines through its territories on the basis of the 'New Order' in Europe. Naturally, Germany took the lion's share: it incorporated into the Reich the northern half of Slovenia. It also took over military control of Vojvodina and did the same with Serbia, bringing German officials alongside the puppet state of the collaborator General Milan Nedić. The southern half of Slovenia was incorporated into Italy. Ljubljana became an Italian province, with its own licence plate symbol, and Italianized Slovenians became subject to the military draft, to Italian taxes, and to all other obligations pertaining to that undesired nationality. Sibenik, Dubrovnik, Kotor, and Split, along with the entire Dalmatian coast, the islands, and the region of Carniola, also became Italian to all intents and purposes. Kosovo and a section of Macedonia were made part of the Kingdom of Albania (whose crown already belonged to the Italian king, Victor Emmanuel III). The entire Banat was absorbed by Romania, and the region of Baka by Hungary, while the rest of Macedonia was awarded to Bulgaria.

Thanks to Ante Pavelić and his Ustachi, only Croatia enjoyed special treatment. It was transformed into an independent state comprising Bosnia, Herzegovina, and part of Dalmatia as well as all of Croatia proper. The crown of the new kingdom was offered to a prince of the House of Savoy. All power, however, lay in the hands of Pavelić, who would obey now the Italians, now the Germans, according to the ups and downs of power struggles.

Only Montenegro was left. This poor, mountainous region had no strategic value at all. But it was the birthplace of Elena, Queen of Italy, so its future was of interest to the House of Savoy. Until this point, Victor Emmanuel III had not shown any interest in acquiring new territories in the Balkans. He distrusted Slavs and he could foresee only difficulties. When dealing with the first disagreements with Zagreb over the partitioning of Dalmatia, the Italian foreign minister Galeazzo Ciano wrote in his diary: 'The King believes that the less of Dalmatia we take, the less troubles we will have. *If it were not for certain understandable sentimental reasons, I would be favourable to ceding even Zara to the Croatians.'* Pressured by his wife, however, the Italian king in turn pressured Ciano and Mussolini to ensure that the Kingdom of Montenegro would be reconstituted and that its crown would be given to Prince Michael, son of Danilo Petrovi, Elena's brother. On this matter, Ciano noted in his diary: 'The King insists on the restoration of the monarchy. I fear this will create some troubles, but the Duce has already come on side and I do not want to be the spoiler. A nephew of the Queen will be king of Montenegro, a young man the Duce described as *the son of few and poor parents*. He lives in Germany, in Lobau, in obscurity and famine, or close to it.'

In the end, Michael did not become king. Montenegro's monarchists rejected this proposal and insisted instead on having Elena herself as their queen. This proposal, although supported by Ciano, found Victor Emmanuel unsure and stubborn. So nothing was done, and Montenegro remained without a monarch.

By the early summer of 1941, the new arrangements for the ex-Yugoslavia were encounting their first difficulties. Everywhere, but especially in the areas controlled by Italy, the first sparks of resistance were beginning to flash. Partisan groups of various ethnic and political stripes – and in fact often hostile to one another – began to make their presence felt through ambushes and acts of sabotage. The resistance began in Montenegro itself.

As Giacomo Scotti writes, the Italian occupation forces had at first found support among the old nationalists, who saw the Kingdom of Montenegro being reborn under Italian protection. Then, on 13 July 1941, while in Rome and in Cetinje the authorities were discussing who should sit on the throne, a general insurrection broke out. Within a few weeks, the Italian troops had been forced to fall back to their strongholds of Cetinje, Niksic, and Podgorica. Ciano wrote in his diary: '14 July. Riots in Montenegro. Gun battles. The capital is isolated. We have sent forces from Albania.' Three days later: 'The Montenegro uprising is constantly gaining strength. If it did not have a profoundly bitter meaning, it would be grotesque: there is war between Italy and Montenegro! Let us hope our soldiers can resolve it without having to ask for German help.' And this was only the beginning.

The Ustachi Unleashed against Serbians and Jews

By 6 April 1941, when Operation Punishment began, the Croatians had already risen against the hated Serbian government. Now they helped the advancing Italian and German forces, welcoming them as liberating armies. Then the slaughter commenced, just as it had throughout the centuries every time one of the two largest Slavic ethnic groups was able to gain the upper hand against the other. 'Ethnic cleansing' is not a tragic new development of modern times; it has long been a constant in the relations among the various groups in the Yugoslavian mosaic.

The abyss of hatred that divided Croatians and Serbians was ancient and ran deep. Only the spoken language joined the two people; their histories, cultures, and customs were completely antithetical. They even used different alphabets (the Croatians the Latin one, the Serbians the Cyrillic). Perhaps most important, the Croatians were Catholics, the Serbians were Orthodox. At the end of the First World War, when the borders of the new nation of Yugoslavia were being drawn at Versailles, the Croatians had done all they could not to be included in this artificial political construct. They had even drawn up insurrection plans with Gabriele D'Annunzio after his Fiume escapade and his founding of the Regency of the Carnaro. During the interwar years, Serbian abuses of the Croatians had been relentless and insulting. It can be no surprise that as soon as they saw the chance, the Ustachi would begin to take revenge. And the ferocity of that revenge would quickly beggar the imagination.

Having been recognized by Hitler as Italian *Lebensraum* – that is, as vital Italian living space – Croatia, now led by Poglavnik Ante Pavelić, offered its crown to the House of Savoy. No one in the Italian royal house wanted it: the risks were too obvious. Furthermore, the Ustachi government had issued a decree that divested the monarchy of all authority and rendered it a mere figurehead, as Pavelić himself acknowledged.

But this problem needed to be solved, if only not to disappoint the expectations of the powerful German ally. Following dynastic prece-dence, the king designate should have been Duke Amedeo d'Aosta, who at that moment was Viceroy of Ethiopia and engaged in defending the Italian Empire against the British. Since it was impossible for him to return to Italy, the crown fell on his younger brother, Aimone, Duke of Spoleto, who would have expected anything from life but to assume the crown of Zvonimir, the last king of medieval Croatia (d. 1089), and to change his name to Tomislav II.

At that time, Aimone was a brilliant naval officer. He commanded the Naval Department at La Spezia, where he was very popular in the city and much loved by his associates. When he learned that he had been named King of Croatia, he confided to some of his most trusted colleagues that he thought this nomination was a bad joke by his Savoy cousin. He accepted the post out of a sense of duty, while swearing to his men that he would never set foot in Zagreb, not even for the coronation. And so he did not.

In the rest of Yugoslavia, the Germans were carrying out harsh reprisals in an effort to liquidate the two main resistance movements (the still fledgling Communists led by Tito, and the more powerful Chetniks, that is, the monarchist Serbians, led by General Draža Mihajlović). In Croatia, the Ustachi were far more ruthless than even the Nazis. The ethnic cleansing they carried out struck Serbians, Moslems, and Jews indiscriminately. They conducted unspeakable massacres and set up concentration camps (the most notorious one being Jasenovac) that quickly evolved into extermination camps following the German model.

Nearly all the villages of the Serbian minority in Croatia were razed and their inhabitants uprooted. It is impossible to determine how many died during this extermination campaign. According to estimates by the Orthodox Church, the Ustachi in their first year in power were killing two thousand Serbians every day. According to calculations made by a committee of the U.S. Senate, the Serbian victims numbered between 300,000 and 500,000. According to the Yugoslav government, they numbered 700,000, but this report does not mention that the figure includes many who fell victim to Tito's partisans.

The Ustachi were certainly the most ferocious, but the other combatants in the region were not much kinder. For example, Tito's Communist partisans treated the Chetniks the same as German or Italian soldiers to the point that in the end, they drove the Chetniks to side with the invaders. And the Chetniks gave as good as they got. They killed Croatians without distinction, and when given the opportunity, they also killed Moslems in Bosnia. In short, this was a war that pitted everyone against everyone and in which the worst off were the Jews and the Moslems, who were caught in the middle and treated without pity by everyone else.

The atrocities perpetrated in those years are indescribable. An Italian diplomat visiting the Poglavnik in Zagreb reported that he saw a room full of bloody scraps, which he mistook for a tangled mass of snails. 'They are eyes ripped from the Serbians,' an escort explained. Gian Nicola Amoretti, aide-de-camp to Aimone/Tomislav, reported than near Sarajevo, the Ustachi had captured some starving Chetniks. They were offered some meat; then, after the meal, an Ustachi entered the room and showed them the head of a child. 'Do you recognize him?' he asked. 'He's my son!' screamed in horror one of the prisoners. To which the Ustachi responded: 'Did you like his meat?'

The Croatians used to throw the bodies of the Serbians they killed into the Sava River, which would carry them to the Danube and then down towards Belgrade. One summer day, in Belgrade, a large raft was seen floating by with a couple of newlyweds on it, a Catholic priest, and a dozen dinner guests. A large banner carried these words: 'Bračno Putovanje za Crno More' (Honeymoon on the Black Sea). The German soldier who brought it ashore discovered that the passengers had been stabbed to death and nailed to the planks. It was impossible, however, to determine who had perpetrated this crime, part of the pitiless ethnic war between Serbians and Croatians.

In the territories newly annexed to Italy, the Fascist authorities began the process of denationalization already underway in Istria – suppression of the local press and of cultural and sports clubs; Italianization of surnames and signs; obligatory use of the Italian language and of the Roman salute; and all the other antifreedom measures that in time would become excuses for harsh and unjustified reprisals against the Italians of Istria and Dalmatia.

Notwithstanding the behaviour of the Italian civil government, Italian military authorities tried hard to maintain a correct demeanour. The Germans were encouraging the actions of the Ustachi against Serbians, Jews, and Moslems; the Italian military were unable to remain indifferent when confonted with such atrocities. In July 1941, the Italian ambassador in Zagreb, Antonio Casertano, informed Mussolini that Italians soldiers were frequently clashing with German and Ustachi soldiers 'because our soldiers give obvious and constant proof of their sympathy for Jews and Serbians, protecting them from relentless persecutions.' General Ambrosio, commander of the Italian Second Army, reported to the High Command that 'from the month of June on, the presence of Italian troops is not well viewed, especially because they represent an unwelcome witness to the savage slaughter that even honest Croatians are ashamed of.' In Italian Dalmatia, the local authorities offered asylum to the Jewish refugees that were flooding their region.

'German Blood' Becomes Precious

With the war going badly everywhere for the Italians, Rome was losing influence with the Croatian government. Favoured by Ante Pavelić, who was always ready to side with the strongest, the Germans were taking steps to strengthen their political influence in Croatia. The 'experts' of Volksdeutsche Mittelstelle (VOMI) now arrived in Yugoslavia. VOMI had been established by Alfred Rosenberg, the theorist of racism, for the purpose of advancing 'research on and a return to German blood purity.' To this end, it set out to identify 'pure Aryans of German origin' who had mixed with the local population and to promote their re-Germanization. To achieve this goal, the 'experts' resorted to complicated and outright fanciful methods. They examined geneological records dating back to 1785, and they studied migration patterns. They took body measurements and considered the physical appearance of 'candidates,' and so forth. So it happened that unsuspecting illiterate farmers, completely unaware of their past, found themselves classified among the Volksdeutsche – that is, among those of German extraction – with the advantages and disadvantages that came with belonging to this group.

Encouraged by Pavelić, who claimed for his people a 'Runic' origin, VOMI's 'experts' gathered in Croatia a rich harvest of Volskdeutsche. This enabled the German administration to infiltrate the country even though it was part of the Italian Lebensraum. The Ustachi had never loved the Italians and considered it an honour to become 'nearly German.' The Germans permitted them to wear a swastika badge on their uniform, and allowed them to include a declaration of loyalty to the Führer in their oath of loyalty to the Poglavik.

Protected by the Germans, the Croatian Volksdeutsche grew rapidly in number and acquired so much political influence that they placed at risk the survival of the Poglavnik himself, who, unfortunately for him, had no German blood. Then, after the conquest of the Ukraine, Hitler began making plans to transfer there, *en masse*, all the Volskdeutsche the Germans had located in the Balkans. With the prospect of forced removal to the Ukraine, it became inadvisable to claim German blood, so, many neo-Volksdeutsche hastened to rediscover their Slavic roots.

A Yugoslavian Novelty: Partisan War

Victor Emmanuel III had been correct to foresee that the partitioning of Yugoslavia would bring Italy nothing but trouble. Between the days of easy conquest in April 1941 and the days of the Italian defeat after 8 September 1943, the Yugoslavian venture degenerated quickly into a string of rebellions, oppressions, ambushes, sabotages, massacres, and harsh reprisals, all of which only deepened ancient hatreds and resentments. For all of this, the innocent Italian population that had settled centuries earlier in Venezia Giulia would end up paying the bill.

Not even the Germans had foreseen the consequences of their Balkan campaign, which Hitler had launched in a moment of rage. Guerrilla war – a new way of waging war that would quickly prove its worth – was not even discussed in the military academies of the time. That a people might rise in arms against an invading army was considered impossible. In France, in Poland, and in other Axis-occupied countries, the civil populations had resigned themselves to their new situation; they simply hoped the Allied armies would later settle the conflict.

Yugoslavia was an exception. It is ironic that the only people in Europe without a common history and without a common idea of the state, a people sharply divided by ancestral hatreds, found the resolve to strike back against what was for a time the most powerful army in the world. But they did, and this perhaps reveals the measure of their ferocious fighting spirit and of their arrogant pride.

According to the official history, there was only one Yugoslav resistance – the one led by the Croatian Josip Broz, alias Marshal Tito. Tito, however, became its leader only later, after he had liquidated all of those fighters who would not accept his leadership and his ideology. He was able to do so thanks to the protection of Stalin and to second thoughts from Winston Churchill, and later with the help of the Americans. In the beginning, however, the Yugoslav guerrilla war against the Germans was carried out by a variety of groups, all of them spontaneously created and all of them hostile to one another. Foremost among them were the Chetniks, ferocious warriors led by the Serbian general Draža Mihajlović.

On 18 April 1941, the Chetniks (from *ceta*, meaning troop, battalion, cohort) answered the call from Mihajlović, who refused to recognize the capitulation of the Yugoslav army. A few weeks later, while camped in the mountains of Ravna Gora, they were joined by a British military mission, which besides bringing greetings from Churchill, air-dropped into that region enormous quantities of arms, munitions, food, and medical supplies.

The Chetniks spread quickly throughout Yugoslavia until they resembled an actual army. By 1943 they had nearly 350,000 men under command. They were savage fighters, and their appearance reflected this. Although armed with modern machine guns, they also carried long daggers thrust into their wide belts (they often used these daggers in mortal combat with the hated Ustachi). As a sign of their vows, they let their beards and hair grow. In the centre of the Chetnik flag there was a skull.

The Chetnik officers came from the ranks of the disbanded Yugoslav army and from the nobility faithful to Peter II. Most of the fighters were Serbian shepherds and woodsmen, but there were also Montenegrins, Slovenians, and Bosnians, as well as others faithful to the monarchy. They were rough and violent people who applied to their enemies the same treatment their enemies applied to them. As a rule, they took no prisoners.

Draža Mihajlović was their undisputed military leader. One of his key aims was to reunify Yugoslavia as a federal state 'expanded to those territories where Serbians, Croatians, and Slovenians live ... up to the natural border of the Tagliamento River.' As Pier Arrigo Carnier tells it, Mihajlović was a daring and combative man. He believed in the dominant historical role of Serbia, and he shared the belief held throughout the Balkans that Serbians were the best soldiers in the world. His blind faith in this secret virtue made him certain he would win the guerrilla war.

Churchill's 'Betrayal'

Toward the end of 1941, after the German invasion of Russia, the first brigades of Tito's partisans entered the war in Yugoslavia. For some time, the Chetniks and the Communists operated independently, albeit with the common objective of throwing out the invaders, destroying the Ustachi, and reunifying Yugoslavia. The two leaders tried to reach an understanding, but deep ideological differences prevented this. Certain of the support of the Allies (Churchill had been generous with military help and with promises of territory, including, as usual, Venezia Giulia), Mihajlović proudly turned down all of Tito's offers to cooperate. This situation continued for several months, until the equilibrium was broken by what the Chetniks would remember as 'Churchill's betrayal.' This happened in October 1942, when the British prime minister rushed to Moscow to placate Stalin. For some time, the Soviet leader had been demanding that the Allies open a second front in Europe in order to lighten the burden of the war, which so far had fallen completely on the Red Army. (A second front would not be opened until the Allied landing in Normandy in June 1944.) Churchill sought to calm his furious Soviet ally by agreeing to some of his other requests. Among these was recognition of Moscow's influence in the Balkans; this meant abandoning Mihajlović in favour of Tito, whom Stalin considered one of his lieutenants.

Soon after, Great Britain recalled all of its military missions to Mihajlović and transferred them to Tito's High Command. One of the men in these missions was Churchill's own son, a captain. The Americans, uneasy about making such a sensational reversal, remained with Mihajlović. Harold Macmillan would write in his memoirs: 'The Americans aid the right wing of the Yugoslav guerrillas, and we the left wing.' But in the end, even President Roosevelt bent to Stalin's extortion, and Mihajlović found himself completely isolated.

All of this was a harsh blow to the Chetniks. The groups scattered, and Mihajlović, whom the Communists immediately fingered as a traitor, sought refuge with his last supporters in the mountains of Ravna Gora. Bloody clashes between the two partisan groups followed, much to the benefit of the Germans. Thousands of Chetniks, out of hatred for the Communists, opted to collaborate with the Axis forces, reaching a kind of accord whereby they agreed to fight only against *Titini*, and not against the Allies. This would not be enough to save the Chetniks. Churchill and Stalin would seize on this de facto collaboration to distance themselves from Mihajlović and his movement.

Mihajlović never reduced himself to making pacts with the Germans. He continued the fight with his last supporters even after the war ended. His death is still shrouded in mystery. It is known that he was captured in 1946 by Tito's agents and was later shot. The gravesite has never been revealed, to ensure that it does not become a shrine.

'Not a Tooth for a Tooth, but a Head for a Tooth'

For the Italian occupation forces scattered throughout the Yugoslav muddle, the troubles feared by Victor Emmanuel III soon manifested themselves, and were worse than he predicted. Until 8 September 1943, the entire Balkan Front (from the recently annexed Slovenia to Greece) would require more Italian troops than any other during the war – more than 650,000 men, 270,000 in Slovenia and Croatia alone.

In the early postwar period, Yugoslavia levelled various accusations against Italy. Most of these were for the sake of presenting the later massacres of Italians as phenomena of popular justice. For example, there was the accusation that during the occupation, Italy committed atrocities. In the years right after the war, the Yugoslav media did not hesitate to brand the Italian soldiers as no better than the Germans and the Ustachi. In fact, the Italian soldiers behaved far better than this. Naturally, after the situation grew especially tense, there were some serious excesses, but in the early days, even the Fascists expressed their horror at the crimes committed by the Germans and the Ustachi. 'Plunders, rapes, murders are the order of the day,' Ciano noted with outrage in his diary. Around the same time, the Provincial Secretary of the Fascist Party of Trieste, Federale Emilio Grazioli, Commissary for Slovenia, lamented the cruelties and abuses of the Nazis. For their part, the Germans accused their Italian allies of 'clear and constant proof of sympathy' toward the Serbians and the Jews, whom the Italians protected from Ustachi persecution and helped relocate, with their goods, to the Italian zone.

Even when the fighting became more intense and attacks against Italian soldiers increased (who were subdivided and scattered in a myriad of small unit often indefensible), many officers hesitated to carry out the draconian reprisal measures ordered by the High Command in order to conform with German practice. The soldiers were highly ambivalent about serving as policemen, and many refused to follow orders. Generally, the harsh punishments reserved for saboteurs were not applied.

The Italian units found themselves trapped inside a civil war that pitted everyone against everyone. As a result, they got lost in a tangle of tribal, ideological, and religious hatreds that no one could unravel. Croatian Ustachi and Serbian Chetniks who had crossed over to the Axis could not be placed side by side to fight against Tito's partisans because they would immediately begin shooting at each other. In Gospic in November 1941, the Italian Alpini were compelled to open fire against their own Ustachi allies in order to prevent a massacre of Serbians.

As the fighting intensified, the Italians found themselves sucked into a spiral of reprisals. Roundups, deportations, and executions followed, and villages were razed. In 1941 in the district of Sibenik, 240 hostages were shot; in June 1942, again in Dalmatia, 470 civilians were shot in reprisal during a roundup conducted by the Sardinian Grenadiers and the Macerata Division. In the winter of 1942 in Slovenia, in Ljubljana – a forbidden city after sundown on account of the constant assaults – 103 people were executed.

For the partisans, sabotage and ambushes were standard practice. On 27 November 1942, in Montenegro, an Italian column was overrun after a day of fighting. The survivors were shot; the officers were chopped into pieces with axes and were thrown into a mountain crevasse. This event is noted because it was the first time the Yugoslavs were caught using a mountain crevasse as a burial pit. Later, however, it would come to light that as early as December 1941, one hundred Alpini from the Pusteria Regiment had suffered the same fate.

The Alpini took the heaviest casualties in the fighting because their corps was the best suited for mountain operations. That said, the most hated Italian soldiers were the Black Shirts – the Italian equivalent of the German SS. The *Titini* saw them as the speartip of Italian repression and as their ideological archenemy, and showed them no mercy. In March 1942, around one hundred survivors from a Black Shirt battalion destroyed in Dalmatia were pushed into Lake Popovo Polje and deliberately suffocated in the mud along the store. Shortly after, General Alessandro Pirzio Biroli, the Italian commander in Montenegro, reported: 'The insurrection is fed by hatred against Fascists. This explains why the rebels did not spare the men of the 108th Legion of Black Shirts captured in the fighting, while all the soldiers in grey-green uniforms were spontaneously set free.'

The behaviour of the Italian soldiers was also a function of the mindset of their immediate commanders. Fortunately, the Italian army did not embrace that iron discipline of the sort which shaped its allies. Each soldier obeyed his conscience more than his orders. For example, not everyone obeyed the drastic 'Circular 4' issued by General Mario Roatta, commander of the Second Army, in which he decreed that 'rebels must not be treated according to the formula of *a tooth for a tooth*, but that of *a head for a tooth*.' Some generals, however, showed themselves to be harsher than the Fascists. A bulletin from General Mario Robotti, commander of the XI Army Corps: 'Wherever you go, get rid of all the people that might shoot you in the back. It is understood that the regulation on internment does not void the regulation on firing squads.'

Evidently displeased by the reprehensible humanitarianism of his men, Robotti scolded General Ruggero, who had just mentioned the arrest of seventy-three suspects: 'Be clear on how you deal with the suspects, because it seems to me that out of seventy-three suspects, not to find one to make an example of, is not good enough. What does regulations 4 C say? Conclusion: one does not kill enough!' From another report: 'In Primosten, south of Sibenik, the Navy men and Bersaglieri have received the order to kill everyone they find. The soldiers, of their own initiative, have not killed anyone, neither women nor children.'

Clearly, there is no shortage in this story of high points and low points, of reversals and duplicity. Everyone's hands are bloody, including the Italians'. In some districts, the Italians protected the civilian population; in others, they shot them. In Ljubljana, two young students were arrested by an Italian officer simply for glaring at him on the street. Later, that same officer was approached by two Slovenian friends, who begged him to intervene to save the life of two young friends of theirs. When they explained to him what had happened, he understood that they were speaking of the two youths he himself had arrested. Repenting his action, he searched all the police stations for them, only to discover that the soldiers to whom the youths had been turned over had already freed them on their own initiative.

At the same time, there are plenty of examples of stupid or criminal abuses of power. Groups of farm women were assaulted in the marketplace because they were unable to sell their produce in Italian; civilians were whipped for keeping their hats on in front of an Italian flag; students with antifascist leaflets in their pockets were imprisoned and tortured for weeks and sometimes brutally killed by Fascist militia or policemen.

A day did not go by without brutalities by one side or the other. Not all Italian soldiers were good, and not all Fascists were bad. The Commissioner for Slovenia, the Fascist Emilio Grazioli, would turn to General Gambara to complain about the harsh treatment meted out to those who had been interned in Italian prison camps ('absolutely all of them reveal the most severe evidence of lack of activity and starvation'), only to be told: 'It is logical and correct that concentration camp should not mean fattening camp. Sick person = quiet person.'

High points and low points, as we have said. Mussolini himself was involved in a humanitarian episode. The historian Renzo De Felice recounts that the Duce had been swamped for some time by German requests for the 'return' of Yugoslav Jews who had sought refuge in Italian-occupied areas. He had tried everything to avoid giving in to German pressure. First, through a bureaucratic subterfuge, he nullified his consent. Then he tried to delay everything indefinitely with the excuse that a census was required to determine how many of these Jews 'belonged' to the Germans. Finally, he ordered that all of these Jews be shipped to the Dalmatian island of Arbe to avoid the possibility that some changes being suggested to the occupation areas in favour of Croatia might favour their capture. The Germans, smelling a rat, arrived at a plan to transfer them by sea to Trieste and from there to

Germany, but Rome let it be known that the ships necessary for this were unavailable. The duplicity of the Italians irritated the Germans so much that their complaints forced Mussolini to give in: the Jews on Arbe would be handed over. Then, immediately after, speaking with General Robotti, Mussolini confessed his disappointment: 'Minister Ribbentrop has come to Rome and has bothered me for hours insisting that Hitler wants at all costs that the Yugoslav Jews be handed over. I muttered this and that, but because he would not go away, eventually I had to agree in order to get rid of him. But you make up all the excuses you want so as not to hand over a single Jew.'

An Italian-style solution: morally squalid, but one that saved the lives of many. The history of the Italian occupation of Yugoslavia is full of these painful contradictions.

8 September Reversed

'What will the Germans do now?' This anguished question, on every Italian's lips on the evening of 8 September 1943, when Marshall Badoglio surprised everyone by announcing the signing of the armistice, was immediately submerged in Venezia Giulia by another, more dramatic question: 'What will the *Slavs* do now?'

Their fears were more than justified. Relations between the two populations, already tense because of the occupation, had reached the breaking point with the war's most recent events. These had been disastrous for Italy, but favourable for the partisan struggle, which had now gained a foothold inside Italy. During the 'forty-five days of the Badoglio government' that followed Mussolini's fall on 25 July 1943, no attempt was made to lessen the difficulties of occupation and to break the parallel between being Italian and being Fascist, a failure for which the Italians of the Julian provinces would pay a heavy price in the coming years. The Italian government continued instead to emphasize nationalism, and as a result Slavic nationalists would soon turn against Italy.

Aside from the Germans, who had already made plans to seize the Italian-occupied territories, Tito's partisans and Pavelić's Ustachi took early advantage of the chaos in the Italian armed forces brought about by the armistice. The partisans pounced on the scattered Italian forces and on the abandoned armouries in order to capture weapons, munitions, and military vehicles – a colossal bounty that would allow Tito to outfit an army. Meanwhile, the Ustachi gobbled up 'the Croatian lands on the Adriatic.'

On the evening of 8 September, Pavelić, delighted to be free of Italy's formal 'protection,' declared war on Badoglio's Italy. Hitler, he declared, had recognized 'to the independent state of Croatia its rights not only to Dalmatia, but to the cities of Zara and Fiume.' Large anti-Italian demonstrations were quickly organized in Zagreb and other Croatian cities.

On the eve of the surrender, nearly 300,000 Italian soldiers were stationed in Venezia Giulia, Slovenia, Croatia, and Dalmatia. They belonged to the Second and Eighth armies. The Second was led by General Robotti (after Roatta had been called to head the Army High Command), the Eighth by General Italo Gariboldi. The Eighth was the ex-ARMIR that had returned from the disastrous Russian campaign. It included the glorious Alpini divisions Julia, Cuneense, and Tridentina, but these were still being reorganized and lacked heavy armaments.

Even in the climate of confusion and uncertainty that enveloped the complex manoeuvres to reach an armistice without the Germans finding out about it, the Italian High Command had been planning operations to protect the eastern frontier and to expedite the return to Italy of troops stationed in Yugoslavia. General Gastone Gambara was chosen to carry out these plans and was quickly summoned to Rome from Slovenia, where he commanded the XI Corps of the Second Army. On 5 September, having been informed of what was about to happen, Gambara received the order to return to base and set up a special force consisting of units from the two armies deployed there 'so as to carry out special operations in the event of a foreseen German attack on Venezia Giulia.' The general had, above all, to guarantee Italian possession of Trieste, Pola, and Fiume so as to facilitate a possible Allied landing in the north Adriatic.

Gambara would later recall that on receiving his orders he requested at least ten days' lead time. He was told that the armistice would not be officially announced before 12 September, so he would have the time necessary for his task. But events came to a head much more quickly. Gambara left Rome by car in the afternoon of 8 September and was informed of the armistice as he was passing by Foligno. Although disconcerted by the news, he continued his journey by air and on the morning of 9 September he reached Fiume. When he arrived there, he found the situation distressing: on orders from Rome, all Italian naval units had left the harbours of Pola and Fiume and were heading for Malta. These ships included the corvette *Baionetta*, which at Pescara on the evening of 9 September would take aboard the royal family, Badoglio, and the top ranks of the Italian military in flight toward Brindisi. The land units, lacking both orders and commanders, were beginning to fall apart. Many had already laid down their weapons; others were engaged in armed encounters, now with the Germans, now with the Ustachi, now with the partisans. In Fiume and Pola, the first incidents of looting were being reported. In the meantime, the Italian population, in a panic, was begging for protection from the Slavic threat, which was already building.

In all this confusion, thwarted in his efforts to organize an armed resistance, closed in as he was between the *Titini*, the Ustachi, and the Germans, General Gambara, as the entire population of Istria would later do, opted for what he considered the lesser of the three evils: the Germans. He would claim later that he had been obliged to make this choice, considering the dangers represented by the Slavs, 'who would certainly not have spared the tens of thousands of Italian citizens living in Fiume.' A few days later, when most of his men were on the road to internment in Germany or struggling to return to Italy by any means available, Gambara was taken to Trieste under German escort. He later joined the Italian Social Republic, in which he would hold a post in the High Command of the republican army established by Marshal Rodolfo Graziani.

The Panslavic National Front

From the very beginning of the guerrilla war, Communist cadres had been preparing Yugoslavia and the Julian provinces for 'liberation.' The party officials, some of whom were Italian, carried out propaganda relentlessly and with great skill. In factories and shipyards, where the Italian presence was strong, they focused on the idea of international labour, on self-government by the people, on the Soviet Union as the beacon of socialism, and on Tito's new Yugoslavia as an outpost of the expanding socialist world. In the countryside, among the Slavic farmers, the message was different: it touched the emotional chords of national deliverance, and it promised listeners that for the people of Istria the day of redemption and vengeance was at hand, that the Italian and Fascist landlords would soon be evicted, and that everyone would live happily and joyfully in the greater Yugoslavia that Tito would finally reconstitute within its borders.

Because it would have been otherwise difficult to keep the huge and fractious resistance movement united, the party's propagandists generally were silent on the usual class struggle and internationalist themes that characterized Communist propaganda elsewhere. Instead, it appropriated and trumpeted without shame the pan-Slavic vindication; this, along with the desire for revenge against the Italians, was the only glue capable of uniting the multiple and contradictory elements of Yugoslav thinking. The propagandists of the Yugoslav Communist Party found the soil extremely fertile to their infiltration work, thanks to the forced nationalization policies carried out by Rome, and to the work of the Catholic clergy, who continued to instill a deep sense of nationalism in the Slavic population.

Gaetano La Perna, one of the most balanced Istrian historians, notes that it was the Slavic clergy, whose seminaries were hotbeds of the movement, and whose parishes and sacristies were used as safe havens, that enabled party activists to breathe life into that broad, pan-Slavic national front which would subsequently serve as the party's springboard into power.

Relations between the Italian Communist Party and its Yugoslav counterpart were much more problematic. Rooted deeply in the Julian cities and above all in the district of Monfalcone, the Italian party was viewed by the Yugoslav party as blocking its efforts to penetrate those territories. Clearly, the national question was dividing them. This issue was the focus of long discussions in the clandestine meetings between delegations of the two parties. At the end of these meetings, they would usually conclude that the territorial question 'would be put on the table only after the final victory over nazifascism' and that naturally it would be resolved by the 'brother' parties, keeping in mind the rights of the minorities and the self-government of the people. Meanwhile, the Yugoslavs continued their nationalist campaign, relentlessly pounding out the message that the Slavic people had a claim to see Venezia Giulia, Dalmatia, and Carinthia united in the common motherland. Their favourite slogan, drawn from one of Tito's declarations: 'We do not want what belongs to others, but we do not give away what is ours.'

Often the leaders of the two parties asked for 'enlightment' from headquarters in Moscow, but the answers that came back were either ambiguous or favourable to the annexationist policies of Yugoslavia. At the same time, both in the grassroots and in the leadership of the Italian Communist Party in Venezia Giulia, the Slavic penetration was felt ever more strongly, endorsed above all by the myth of the Soviet Union and by Tito presenting himself as its favourite son. And so the belief took hold that Italians in the region would be better off in a socialist Yugoslavia than in an Italy destined to be dominated by hated imperialism.

The Italian Communist Party of Trieste Leaves the National Liberation Committee

The political line of the Trieste section of the Italian Communist Party changed in a sensational way when the federation's leadership recalled its representative to the National Liberation Committee, which was composed of representatives of all Italian anti-Fascist parties in the region. This is what happened: during a clandestine meeting, the representative of the Italian Communist Party of Trieste asked the committee to welcome also the representative of the Slovenian Communist Party and to declare officially that the Julian population, including its Italian members, wished to unite with 'the new Yugoslavia of Tito.' The answer of the National Liberation Committee could only be negative, and, as a result, the Triestinian Communists abandoned the Italian committee and joined the Yugoslav National Liberation Committee. This had major repercussions within the National Liberation Committee for Northern Italy, which was directing the clandestine struggle in Italy; however, the Italian Communist Party, represented by Luigi Longo, did not repudiate its Triestinian comrades. On the contrary – a while later, in a memo drafted by its central committee (meant to be 'top secret,' but quickly released to the public by the Yugoslavs), it recognized the need to place all Italian partisan units operating in the Julian region under Slavic command and to accept 'the annexation of Trieste and of the seacoast of Slovenia as an inevitable fact of history.'

The Italian Communist Party maintained this policy throughout the war, but always showed itself ready to be proactive when it came to supporting Tito's demands. Only after the war was over and the Julian question began to boil did the Communist ministers in the Tripartite government approve the declaration that Trieste was 'a city unquestionably Italian.' But the party itself hesitated to do this, and did not change its formal position until 28 June 1948, when, much to the relief of Triestinian Communists, the Moscow headquarters of the Cominform expelled Tito and his League of Yugoslavian Communists.

The First Wave of *Titini* Descends on Istria

The Yugoslav partisans conquered Istria for the first time immediately after 8 September 1943. This was a rapid and unopposed conquest. According to the Istrian historian Luigi Papa, who at the time was serving in the army in the region, Tito must have been told ahead of

time of the forthcoming Italian surrender. There can be no other explanation for the two events occurring simultaneously. On the night of 8
and 9 September, with the Italian soldiers about to 'discharge' themselves *en masse*, Yugoslav partisan units crossed the frontier. They headed
straight for the Italian barracks and the abandoned Italian armouries to
seize considerable quantities of war materials, which had been left
unguarded. A few Italian commanders put up a sporadic resistance, but
within a few days nothing was left of the extensive network of Italian
garrisons and strongpoints. Only Fiume, Pola, and some other coastal
towns, where the few German soldiers present had taken control of the
situation, were excluded from this Yugoslav occupation.

With the arrival of the Yugoslav soldiers, the Slovenian and Croatian
activists in many towns came out in the open. They were soon joined by
Istrians of Slavic origin and by many Italian anti-Fascist groups, who
considered it vital to join forces with the Yugoslavs to fight Fascism and
the German invader. Yugoslav historians have felt justified in defining
this confused situation as a popular insurrection; in fact, it was nothing
more than an outright military occupation.

In the days that followed, Istria was awash in a sea of flags. To the
evident confusion of the Italian anti-Fascists who had participated in
the 'uprising,' the national flags of Slovenia and Croatia nearly blocked
from sight the few red flags of the proletarian revolution and of international Communism. Some Italians flew the tricolour from their windows, but with only the red band showing, or with a large red star
hurriedly sown onto the white band. The Yugoslavs did not like those
colours and soon made it emphatically clear that displays of the Italian
flag were not welcome. After some muted protest, even the most stal-
wart anti-Fascists accepted that it was better to adapt to the new disposition. Their confusion quickly morphed into serious and well-founded
concern, not to mention a crisis of conscience for all of those Italian anti-
Fascists who had welcomed Tito's forces as liberators.

On 26 September, in Pisino, during a tumultuous assembly at which
only two Italians participated, the separation of Istria from Italy and its
'rejoining' with the Yugoslav 'Motherland' was officially proclaimed.
All of the political, economic, and social laws imposed by the Fascist
regime were declared void. It was also decreed that all Italians who had
moved to Istria after 1918 would be 'given back to Italy,' and that all of
the names and signs that had been forcefully Italianized would be
changed back to their old Croatian forms. The following day, Tito
declared Pisino the capital of Istria (in place of Pola, which was occu-

pied at that time by the Germans). All car licence plates were changed from PL (Pola) to PZ (Pazin-Pisino), and a 'people's tribunal' was established at Pisino. This tribunal would serve as the legal cloak for the horrendous slaughter of Italians that was about to begin in Istria.

This tribunal, composed of three farmers, was presided over by Ivan Motika, a lawyer from Zagreb, who died in his nineties in 1998, just as Italian justice, after a half-century of silence, was making its first efforts to shed some light on the massacre of Italians in Venezia Giulia.

The 'Slavic GPU' Comes into Action

While all of this was happening, Slavic militants helped by local agents were beginning to hunt for Fascists, something that in the final analysis was the same as hunting for Italians. Arrests were carried out by night, but nearly always politely and with the explanation that it was merely a matter of normal controls, so panic was slow to develop. Hundreds of Italians were caught by the net of the 'Slavic Ghepeù,' (GPU) as the Yugoslav secret police were now called (an allusion to its Soviet counterpart). Those arrested were small-time local party officials and secretaries, but also city couriers, civil guards, midwives, postal employees, teachers, landowners, clerks, night watchmen, Carabinieri, and forest rangers. In most cases, any charges levelled at these people derived from their membership in the bourgeoisie, or from their adherence to political ideas that differed from those of the occupying forces. But they all shared the grave fault of being Italian.

In Pisino, those who were arrested were locked in the cellar of the castle of the Montecuccoli, the ancient feudal lords of the area. There, they were subjected to mistreatment, humiliation, and long and exhausting interrogations. Most of those arrested would be liquidated without trial. The few trials that *were* carried out in front of the People's Tribunal were tragic farces. The accused had no right to cite documents in self-defence and no right to a lawyer. The verdict was always guilty, and the sentence was always death, and this was always carried out immediately.

Besides Ivan Motika (who for his 'good work' would enjoy a career in the Yugoslav judiciary and would be elected to Parliament in Belgrade), Gaetano La Perna lists a number of other judge–executioners, who for their cruelty would become famous throughout all of Istria: Ciro Raner, once a student in Bologna, who would become special secretary to the 'right hand' of Tito, the Yugoslav foreign minister, Edward Kardelj; his sisters Nada, Vanda, and Lea, who had careers in the OZNA, Tito's secret police; the ex-milkmaid of Pisino, Tonca Surian; the brothers Stamberga; Giovanni Maretich; Giusto Massarotto, who would later become the representative of the Union of Italians of Istria; Benito Turcinovich, who collaborated with Maretich in sending many Italians to death and who then would be welcomed as an anti-Communist refugee in Italy; Giovanni Colich, called 'the hunchback,' the terror of Barbiana; and many others.

Toward the end of September 1943, the Germans began to reconquer Istria. At that point, the mock trials stopped and summary and multiple executions became much more common. With their wrists tied with barbed wire tightened with pliers, the prisoners were pushed in rows into the pits of the bauxite mines and cut down with sprays of machine-gun fire. Others were lined up on the edge of a *foiba*, a mountain crevasse 100 to 300 hundred metres deep, and tossed into the abyss after they were shot. Often, however, the executioners would kill only the first one in the row; falling into the chasm, he would then drag all his fellow victims down with him. Many of the condemned were tortured and castrated before their execution, others were forced to strip naked in front of their executioners. In coastal areas, mass drownings were used. Again tied one to the other with wire, the victims were carried out to sea on boats and thrown overboard. But the most common method for getting rid of bodies was to throw them into the *foibe*; this was considered the most practical solution and the easiest to hide.

The *Foibe* as Body Pits

Foibe are very common throughout Istria. The mouths of these natural chasms are only a few metres wide and are nearly always hidden by vegetation. Below each mouth lies a vast and torturous abyss that can descend three hundred metres. At the bottom are vast caverns, often crossed by gushing rivers that reach the sea along unknown courses. Between 1943 and 1947, Tito's partisans threw into these pits thousands of human beings, victims of the hatred and the passions of the time. Most of the victims were Italians, but there were also Germans, Ustachi, Chetniks, and even some New Zealand soldiers from the British army. How many? Historians on both sides have often battled over the totals (10,000? 20,000? 30,000?), as if one body more or one body less could change the depth of the horror. There can never be an exact count. Five hundred cubic metres of human remains were recovered from the *foiba* of Basovizza, near Trieste; it was calculated that there must have been two thousand victims there – four per cubic metre. It was impossible to identify the bodies and Yugoslav authorities always refused to cooperate in any way. Besides, they had already taken care to destroy the municipal archives and the census records. To hide how many they killed, they had to ensure that Italians from the 'liberated' towns could not be counted.

Democratic and republican Italy never worried about the fate of its *desaparecidos*. The topic was not 'politically correct,' so it was better left alone. Not surprisingly, the *foibe* of Basovizza and Monrupino (the only two on what is left as Italian territory) were declared merely monuments of national interest, not national monuments, and this not until 1982. Their victims had to wait thirty-five years for a wreath from an Italian head of state.

One Martyr among Many

The death of Norma Cossetto (fig. 5), an Istrian woman from Santa Domenica di Visinada, a small town near Visignano, is one of the many dramatic episodes that exemplify the bestial wave of violence that fell on the Italians of Venezia Giulia, Istria, and Dalmatia after 8 September 1943.

The Istrian historian Antonio Pitamitz recounts that Norma was twenty-three years old and belonged to a family of landowners. Her father had held positions in the local branch of the Fascist party. In the summer of 1943, the young woman was enrolled at the University of Padua as a student of Professor Concetto Marchesi and was writing her bachelor's thesis on the history of Istria. She had chosen the title from the colour of her fertile land, reddened by bauxite deposits: *Red Istria*. Her research was part of an ongoing effort by many to prove, on the basis of centuries of Latin and Venetian presence, the Italianness of those lands which the Slavs were now claiming.

Norma had become a familiar figure among the people in the area. She pedalled her bicycle from one town to the next, visiting city halls and church offices to sift through archives. She threw all her youthful enthusiasm into this research, but she was unable to complete it. On 26 September she was picked up by a 'red squad' of Italian and Croatian Communists and locked up in the old barracks of the Carabinieri of Visignano. Her jailers tried to entice her to join their movement, but

Norma curtly refused. Threats did not work either. So she was transferred to the jail in Antignana, together with some friends and family
members who had also been arrested. There, an agonizing calvary
began for her.

In the days that followed, the young woman was repeatedly tortured.
She was also tied to a table top and repeatedly raped by her jailers. A
woman who lived near the prison building, hearing her cries, found the
courage towards evening to draw near the window. Norma, still tied to
the table, was calling for her parents, for help, for water, for pity. After
days of suffering, the unfortunate girl was taken to the town of Santa
Domenica, where the People's Tribunal quickly condemned her and
twenty-six other people to death. The tomb for all of them was to be the
foiba at Villa Suriani. The condemned were tied together and escorted to
the place of execution by sixteen of Tito's partisans. Norma was too weak
to stand, yet before she was pushed into the chasm the jailers decided to
assault her one more time. Having had their way with her now senseless
body, they cut off her breasts and shoved a stick into her genitals.

Nothing would have been known about Norma's final moments had
chance not played its part. Some time after, the Germans who had
reoccupied that area captured some partisans and learned the truth
from them. The sixteen jailers were identified and captured. Norma's
body was recovered from the *foiba*, which was 136 metres deep. At the
bottom lay also the corpses of her twenty-six companions, along with
those of a dozen Italians killed later. Her remains were brought to the
surface after several hours of distressing work by volunteers led by the
chief of the Pola fire brigade, Arnaldo Harzarich (who would later
recover hundreds upon hundreds of bodies from the *foibe*).

Before burial, Norma's body was laid out in the funeral chapel of the
cemetery of Santa Domenica. As retribution, her assailants were forced
to keep a vigil for her all night long by the light of flickering candles. It
was a funeral wake of terror: the following morning, when the sixteen
Titini were shot by the Germans, three had gone mad.

Norma's family suffered seven other *infoibati*. After the war, in her
memory, the University of Padua conferred on her the *laurea honoris
causa*. Someone objected that she did not deserve that recognition because 'she did not fall for freedom.' However, Professor Marchesi,
although a Communist militant himself, declared that Norma Cossetto
had fallen for the Italianness of Istria and that she deserved this recognition more than anyone else.

The Ritual of the Black Dog

Atrocities of the sort to which Norma Cossetto fell victim were not, unfortunately, the exception, but the rule. All women were raped before being thrown into the *foibe*, and all men suffered unspeakable abuse. The jailers tormented especially those who had been public servants: an old reprimand, a favour denied, an act of arrogance, any of these was enough to condemn someone to death. The most hated were the city couriers, possibly because they delivered tax forms from house to house and collected fines. The *Titini* slaughtered them wholesale.

But the 'red militants' did not split hairs. For them, being Italian was already a fault, and the rest did not matter. Antonio De Bianco was a partisan, yet he ended up in the *foiba* at Tegli simply for defending his Italian origins. Nicola Carmignani also was a Communist, but he suffered the same fate for the same reason. The imagination of the slaughterers knew no bounds: don Antonio Particchio, the parish priest of Villa di Rovigno, was found naked in a *foiba* with a crown of barbed wire on his head and his genitals in his mouth. After being beaten to a pulp, Giuseppe Cernecca of Santi Vincenti was led to his place of execution loaded down with a bag of stones. Before throwing him into the *foiba*, they stoned him. Two of his brothers were arrested in Albona and led to their death tied with wire; but before their execution, one jailer, moved to pity, cut the wire and freed the younger of the two. 'Your brother is enough,' he said before letting him go.

In this sombre tragedy, chance sometimes determined one's fate. Giovanni Verzini was arrested because he was mistaken for his uncle, who had the same name. In fact, his uncle was already being held in the castle of Montecuccoli, where prisoners were held while waiting for a 'bus of death' to take them to their final destination. Uncle and nephew met in jail. Two days later, a jailer called out Giovanni Verzini and invited him to leave: 'You are free,' he declared. 'You can go home.' The young man begged his uncle not to reveal the switch: 'I am newly wed, let me run to see my wife, you are single, you can wait another day.' They were unaware that the *Titini* used this trick to deceive the condemned so as not to alarm them. And so the young man ended up in the *foiba* in place of his uncle, who a few days later was liberated by the Germans.

Chance did not help those on one 'bus of death' to the '*Foiba* of the Pigeons' near Vines. While they were waiting for death at the edge of the chasm, a German mobile column passed nearby. Hearing the engines, some of the prisoners screamed for help. The *Titini* shut them up, threatening them with their guns, then killed them one by one with their daggers so as not to make a sound (fig. 7).

To hide the victims and prevent their identification, the killers usually undressed them. They also hid the openings of the *foibe* with brushwood, or blocked them with explosive charges. Another macabre ritual characterized these massacres: after the victims had been thrown into the *foiba*, a live black dog would be thrown on top of them. According to an ancient Balkan legend, the animal, 'with its howls would for all eternity deprive the dead of peace in the world beyond.'

'Freed' by the Germans

'Finally, *they* are coming!' There was not a single Italian in Istria who did not sigh with relief and praise heaven when the Germans appeared. Nowhere else in Europe were German soldiers welcomed as liberators. But they were in Istria. In those October days, still full of summer warmth, the German soldiers with their steel helmets, and camouflage gear and the menacing aura of warrior gods encountered in many villages smiling people who offered them wine and fruit, while church bells rang festively and some rare tricolour that had survived hung from the windows with all three colours in plain view.

After a month of terror, the nightmare was over. Many Istrian Italians would later discover that they had fallen from the frying pan into the fire, but for now they celebrated, and so did many of the local Slavs, who had watched, silent and powerless, while their conationals murdered and pillaged. Everyone, however, worried about those who had disappeared. What had happened to them? Many, the most fortunate, had been freed by the Germans from the makeshift jails that the militias had set up in castles, schools, and churches. But what about the rest?

During the month of terror, there had been no public executions. In fact, whenever the *Titini* arrested someone, they assured their relatives that it was only a simple formality: after interrogation, everyone would be allowed to return home. Few knew the destinations of the night journeys of the 'buses of death,' and few were present at the summary trials conducted by 'the butcher of Pisino,' Ivan Motika, and by other 'judges of the people.' As the Germans drew near and the *Titini* emptied the jails, people still believed the prisoners had been taken somewhere else, to more secure places inland. No one imagined the horrendous slaughter that was being carried out at the *foibe* and at the bauxite mines in the surrounding countryside.

As normality returned, and as the relatives of the *desaparecidos*, continued to agonize, little by little, the harsh truth came to light. The first intimations were raised by isolated farmers, who told of having heard at night the crackling of machine guns and the cries of the victims, which seemed to come from underground and which often continued for hours. No one had the courage to go to their aid. Then came the dramatic testimonies of the fortunate few who had been able to play dead, or who grabbed a branch or a rock outcrop as they fell into the chasm, and thus were able to survive the *foibe*.

This news, still confused, which spoke of massacres, was received at first with astonishment and disbelief, especially in districts that had been occupied by the Germans shortly after 8 September. No one wanted to believe these horror stories, and everyone considered them the products of sick minds or Fascist and Nazi propaganda. Only later, when the recovery operations began, did it become clear that the reality was even worse. The photographs of piles of corpses recovered from the *foibe*, naked, mutilated, and unrecognizable, testified to a dark threat that still hung over all Italians in Istria and Venezia Giulia (fig. 8). These mass executions, which would continue even after the war ended, could not be interpreted (as some people, even in Italy, did in the years that followed) as the Slavs' vengeance for the abuses and torments they had suffered under the Italians. The disproportion of such a revenge was clear to everyone. This had to be something more: it had to be a project of 'ethnic cleansing' carried out deliberately to eradicate Italians from Istria by killing them or by forcing them to flee.

1. English, American, and Yugoslav officers determine that the border between Zone A and Zone B should run along the so-called Morgan Line (1954). This would eventually become the official border between Italy and Yugoslavia.

2. British soldiers drive the yellow stakes into the ground, marking out the border between Zone A and Zone B (1954).

3. Women weep in response to hearing that the Morgan Line situates their homes in Zone B and thus on the Yugoslav side of the border (1954).

4. Italians from Zone B prepare to abandon their homes (1954).

5. Norma Cossetto (d. 1943).

6. Maria Pasquinelli at her trial (1947).

7. Grieving relatives try to identify the bodies retrieved from the *foiba* in Vines (October 1943). Courtesy Istituto Regionale per la Cultura Istriano-fiumano-dalmata, Trieste.

8. The remains of an *infoibato* are laid out in a coffin. Courtesy Istituto Regionale per la Cultura Istriano-fiumano-dalmata, Trieste.

9. The exodus from Pola (February 1947). A young mother and her two children wait on the dock to board the *Toscana*. Courtesy Istituto Regionale per la Cultura Istriano-fiumano-dalmata, Trieste.

10. The bow of the *Toscana*, moored at the dock in Pola (February 1947).

11. Pietro Luxardo (d. 1944). Courtesy Franco and Matteo Luxardo, Torreglia (PD).

12. Piazza Unità d'Italia, Trieste. The official celebrations marking the return of Trieste and Zone A to Italy (26 October 1954).

2

The Adriatisches Küstenland

The Reconquest of Istria

'Wolkenbruch' (Cloudburst) was the code name for the operations carried out by the Germans to reconquer Istria and Dalmatia after Tito's forces marched into them in the wake of 8 September 1943. It was launched at the beginning of October from Trieste, Pola, Fiume, and other coastal centres that the Germans had seized after the Italian surrender. Three armed divisions of SS troops and two divisions of infantry, one of them composed of Turkman soldiers, hurled themselves inland, leaving slaughter and destruction in their wake. The Yugoslav partisans did not even try to resist; they fled *en masse* into the mountains of Croatia and Slovenia, dragging with them hundreds of Italian prisoners, who would be brutally eliminated in the course of the retreat. Partisan losses were very heavy: about 15,000 dead and captured.

The Germans carried out Operation Wolkenbruch so quickly that by 15 October the entire region had been reconquered and transformed into a new province of the Third Reich: the 'Adriatisches Küstenland,' the Adriatic Littoral.

Before 8 September, and even before the fall of Mussolini, the German High Command had been considering the repercussions of an Italian withdrawal from the conflict and how to defend the Reich's southern flank – specifically, the Alpine passes of the Brenner and the lines of communication across Venezia Giulia that reached into the Balkans. The creation of two new Länder dependent on Berlin had already been planned. One of these would consist of the Trentino and Alto Adige, the other of Friuli, Istria, and Venezia Giulia. The Italian surrender accelerated these plans, and the Italian 'betrayal' justified carrying them out. On

10 September, Berlin established the Alpenvorland with Bolzano as its capital, and the Adriatisches Küstenland with Trieste as its capital. The first was entrusted to the Gauleiter of the Tyrol, Franz Hofer, the other to the Gauleiter of Carinthia, the Austrian Friedrich Rainer.

On 12 September, German paratroops liberated Mussolini from the Gran Sasso, which immediately created complications. In Hitler's entourage, everyone was aware of the Führer's feelings towards his Italian friend, and they all feared that if the Duce returned to power, he might persuade the Führer to reconsider his decision to establish two new Länder. Furthermore, the newly established Italian Social Republic made defending the integrity of the motherland a point of honour. In fact, its constitution declared that 'the essential purpose of the foreign policy of the Italian Social Republic will be the unity, independence, and integrity of the Motherland within the maritime and alpine borders marked by nature, by blood sacrifice, and by history.'

But the fears of Hitler's advisers turned out to be unfounded. Mussolini could not move Hitler off his decision, and was forced to submit to yet another humiliation. On 29 September, the German Minister of Propaganda, Joseph Goebbels, noted in his personal diary: 'The Führer is very happy to be able to meet soon with the Duce. Speaking with Gauleiters Hofer and Rainer he said, however, that our politics with respect to Italy must not change. I am very happy about this. I had already feared that the reappearance of the Duce might change things. It seems, instead, that the Führer is determined to persist in his firmness.' Some days later, Goebbels added:

> I approached a serious and important question with the Führer asking him up to what point he intends to expand the territory of the Reich (aside from the Alto Adige and the Adriatic Littoral). According to him, we ought to advance to the borders of the Veneto and the Veneto itself should be included in the Reich in an autonomous form. The Veneto should be willing to accept this condition all the more easily since the Reich, after this victorious war, could provide it with the tourist industry on which Venice puts so much store. I, too, believe such a border to be the only practical and desirable one.

'Trieste Greets Vienna, Vienna Greets Trieste'

On 15 October 1943, the Adriatisches Küstenland was officially founded, consisting of Udine, Trieste, Gorizia, Pola, and Fiume, and including the territories of Buccari (Bakar), Ciabar (Čabar), Casta (Kastav), and Veglia (Krk). The name chosen by the Germans for this new region alarmed the Julian population, which was Italian by sentiment. Adriatisches Küstenland had, in fact, been the name used for that area in Hapsburg times. But this was only the beginning. Rainer openly expressed his intention to make the region once again Austrian, flattering the rich local bourgeoisie who yearned for past imperial glories and good administration and pointing out the contrast between Nazi politics and the anti-Slavic, nationalist politics practised until that time by the Fascist regime. He encouraged seasoned Austrian bureaucrats who had held posts under the Hapsburgs to return *en masse* from Carynthia, and he decreed that German and the Slavic languages would again be official languages on par with Italian, and that knowledge of them would be a prerequisite for employment in the public service. He also encouraged and financed the Slavic press and Croatian and Slovenian cultural associations. In appointing prefects and other authorities, he adopted the practice of placing a Slavic or German substitute next to every Italian government official. All public schools were made multilingual. 'Foreigners' – that is, Italians residing in the Social Republic – now required a passport to travel to Udine or Trieste. All signs of an Italian presence on the Littoral were gradually erased. It was even forbidden to fly the tricolour, and this regulation applied even to the pennants and the ensigns of military detachments of the Italian Social Republic operating alongside German detachments in the region. Even the Italian flags along the border with Croatia were lowered permanently. The work of anti-Italian denationalization took on the character of outright anti-Italian provocation when, for example, the monument in Capodistria to Nazario Sauro, the hero of the First World War, was taken down, with the excuse that the Allies might use it as a ground marker during their aerial attacks. In Gorizia, Slavic elements protected by the SS demolished the monument to the Italian Fallen Soldier with a charge of TNT.

In the operation zones, the German occupiers proved themselves to be as cruel and pitiless as anywhere else; but at least in Trieste, Rainer tried to gain the favour of those who, after twenty years of Fascist government, yearned for the order and efficiency of the Austrian administration. To a degree, he succeeded. As Glauco Arneri writes, in some business circles, people even began to dream that Trieste would return to the glory days of its past.

Continuing with his 'soft' politic, Rainer reopened the halls of the

Palace of Government to the veterans of the First World War who had fought against Italy and who, for many years, had been forced to hide their military decorations. The war amputees and decorated veterans from Trieste who served in the Austrian army could once again display their medals, and the Gauleiter saw to it that sizeable subsidies were granted to them. Every evening, the local radio station transmitted a popular program, *Wien gruesset Triest* (Trieste greets Vienna); the waltzes, polkas, and military marches of their youth filled the Triestinians with nostalgia.

Rainer's approach was welcomed by the bankers and industrialists of Trieste, who had always considered Trieste the chief seaport of Mitteleuropa and who hoped that the war would end with the city once again playing that role.

A Hunter of Jews Lands on the Littoral

In military and security matters, the strongman of Adriatisches Küstenland was SS Gruppenführer Odilo Globocnik. He was born in Trieste in 1904, and in spite of his mixed blood and Slovenian name, had succeeded in acquiring all the marks of 'Aryan purity.' He spoke Italian with a Triestinian accent, but he had been educated in Austria, where his family had moved after the First World War. A Nazi from the very beginning, after the Anschluss he had been named Gauleiter of Vienna. Protected by Himmler – who arranged his promotion from second lieutenant to general in one jump – the Triestinian had had a stunning career in the SS. A dissolute, ambitious, and merciless man, he had distinguished himself in Poland as an expert hunter of Jews. He had participated in the 'euthanasia program' (to eliminate the weak and deformed) and had directed with chilling efficiency the death camp at Treblinka.

Transferred to Trieste with instructions to capture the Jews that the good-natured Fascist administration had saved, Globocnik quickly took control of the military organization as well. Over the protests of the government in Salò, the capital of the Italian Social Republic, he saw to it as soon as he assumed his duties that the citizens of the region would be exempt from military service in the Republic. They could enrol in the Fascist army only as volunteers. And to tell the truth, there were plenty of volunteers, even among those who weren't Fascists; many young men donned the uniform of the National Republican Guard not only to avoid being drafted by the Germans, but also to defend the Littoral for the Italians. The Germans limited themselves to calling up the classes of 1920 to 1928 for 'work duty' in the Todt Organization.

The National Republican Guard was born in the context of the reconstruction of the armed forces of the Italian Social Republic and from the fusion of the Volunteer Militia with the Carabinieri. Its duties included safeguarding the public and fighting partisans. It was under the direct control of the Ministry of the Interior in the Salò government. On the Littoral, however, the National Guard did not last long. To end any interference from the Italians, the German command disbanded it and ordered its members to transfer over to the newly created Territorial Defence Militia. The Carabinieri and the Guardie di Finanza (customs and excise officers) were given other duties. The Territorial Defence Militia worked for the SS and was part of the Landschutz, the territorial police, which also included (with identical responsibilities) the various Slavic formations that had sided with the Germans. It even contained 'legal' Chetniks, Slovenian Domobranci, Catholic Belagardists,[1] Croatian Ustachi, and various groups from other movements that had arisen from the muddle of the Yugoslav civil war. Naturally, they all found it very difficult to get along with one another. The various ethnic groups clashed every day, and blood was often spilled. Yet however divided they were by ancestral hatreds, the Slavic collaborators were always in accord when it came to crushing the Italians. Inspector Giuseppe Gueli, Chief of Police for the Salò Republic, reported: 'Thanks to the German policies of equal standing for all nationalities, Slovenian and Croatians find the way of physically showing their ancestral hatred for Italians.' He concluded: 'Armed to fight against Communist partisans, they direct all their activities, instead, in fighting Italians for being Italian.'

To complete the many-sided and multiethnic picture of the forces active in the Adriatic Littoral, we cannot ignore the other units created by Globocnik. Two of these in particular testified to the weakening of the principle of 'racial purity,' which the Nazis were being forced to abandon because they were running out of 'pure Aryans' to enrol in the SS. One was an SS division of Moslem Bosnian volunteers (who were even allowed to pray toward Mecca twice a day); the other was the 24th Waffen Division SS 'Karstjager' – that is, the 'Hunters of the

---

1 The Domobranci ('Defenders of the Home') and the Belagardists ('White Guards') were armed Slovenian nationalist groups closely tied to the Germans and fiercely opposed to Tito's Communist partisans (translator's note).

Carso' – which included Slovenians, Tyroleans, and Italians from Istria. Some units of this latter group would continue fighting until May 1945, long after all other German forces in Italy had surrendered to the Allies.

The denationalization of the Littoral reached its peak when Globocnik brought into the area of Gorizia, Carnia, and northern Friuli the Cossack army of the collaborationist *ataman* Petr N. Krasnov (author of *From the Imperial Eagle to the Red Flag*). This force consisted of about 15,000 men, and was trailed by their families and a convoy of carts. They were assigned a vast territory newly named Kosakenland.

The Tenth Mas on the Eastern Border

The Tenth Fleet Mas of Junio Valerio Borghese deserves a separate chapter. This was the only Italian unit in the Littoral to retain its Italian national character as well as its autonomy.

Established at La Spezia on 9 September 1943 on the initiative of the Roman prince who headed it, the Tenth gathered around itself, besides many volunteers, some of the veterans of the legendary attacks on the British Mediterranean fleet at Malta, Alexandria, and Gibraltar. Within the structure of the armed forces of the Social Republic, this military formation enjoyed even in Italy a special status that granted it autonomy with respect to both the Salò government and the Germans, who did not interfere with it politically. The historian Renzo De Felice describes it as 'the point of reference for those who, ahead of any Fascist idea, placed the defence of national honour and borders against *all* enemies of Italy, internal as well as external.'

The patriotic character that Borghese was able to instil in the Tenth explains the support it enjoyed especially in Venezia Giulia, where it recruited a number of volunteers of Italian origin.

As Borghese tells it in his own memoirs, the idea of moving his forces to 'the eastern borders of the Motherland' had been suggested to him by an alarming dispatch of 21 August 1944 from the Reuter news agency announcing that the Yugoslav government of Marshal Tito 'demanded all the regions where Slavs lived that were not yet part of Yugoslavia, that is, Gorizia, Trieste, Pola, Fiume, Zara, the islands of Istria and of the Dalmatian coast once belonging to the Austro-Hungarian Empire before the war of 1915–18.' The Reuter item added that Count Carlo Sforza, a minister in the government of the Kingdom of the South, had remarked that 'at least Trieste could remain Italian, perhaps with its port internationalized,' but that Tito's government 'did not want to compromise on absolute Yugoslav sovereignty over the city.'

The arrival of the Tenth, six thousand men strong, all Italian and led by Italian officers, was of course welcomed with great relief by the Italians of the Littoral. The 'Julian Movement' headed by Nino Sauro, son of the hero from Capodistria, which had worked hard in the face of enormous difficulties to keep alive the national spirit, sided enthusiastically with the newcomers. The Germans, however, quickly showed themselves to be hostile.

The presence of an autonomous Italian force in the Littoral did not fit into the denationalization program being advanced by Rainer. In fact, the Germans sought by every means possible to frustrate the actions of the Tenth, raising obstacles against it – some of them humiliating – and provoking many incidents. In Gorizia, for example, they intervened with arms to prevent the flying of the Italian flag in front of the head-quarters of the Tenth, reflecting Rainer's decree against the use of the tricolour anywhere in the region. There followed a sensational free-for-all in which the German soldiers were surrounded and disarmed by the *marò* of the Barbarigo Battalion. The incident ended with the Germans apologizing 'for the deplorable misunderstanding' and the Italians returning their weapons to them.

Various units of the Tenth were later deployed along the Littoral. Each was assigned a historically symbolic name: the company 'Gabriele D'Annunzio' in Fiume and Zara, the company 'Nazario Sauro' in Pola, the battalion 'San Giusto' in Trieste. A school for frogmen was set up at Portorose, a base for minisubmarines at Pola, and a base for assault units on the island of Brioni. Nonetheless, when Captain Borghese arrived in Trieste to carry out a review of his troops, the German authorities ordered him not to leave the city. He disobeyed, and visited Pola and then Fiume, where he was met with an arrest warrant from the Gauleiter. The arrest was not carried out so as to avoid an armed clash, but Borghese was obliged to return to Italy.

Zara's Calvary

In Dalmatia, the situation was much more dramatic than in Istria because of 'the indescribable evil wreaked upon us by our *ally* Croatia,' as Mussolini reported in a note to the Minister of the Interior. Zara had been the principal objective of Allied bombers, which by November 1944, after fifty-four consecutive raids, had reduced it to rubble. The

Dalmatian city had been attacked so relentlessly because Tito had convinced the Allied commanders that Zara was the supply depot for all the German forces in the Balkans. Actually, Zara was of no strategic importance whatsoever; it was not a road junction, it had no armouries, and it was controlled by only a hundred German soldiers. So why destroy it? The answer can be found in a memo cited by the Istrian historian Oddone Talpo, according to whom 'the tragic destruction was prompted by Tito more to erase the traces of centuries of Italianness than for valid strategic reasons.'

In Zara and in Spalato, besides having to defend themselves against the partisans and Allied bombing, Italians also had to confront the Ustachi. After capturing Dalmatia, Ante Pavelić launched a furious anti-Italian campaign. He introduced the kuna alongside the lira, he annulled all debts incurred by Croatian citizens with Italian banks, and he sequestered all goods and businesses belonging to Italians. Subsequently, Italians were deprived of their nationality: to remain in their houses they had to ask for a 'residence permit.' They were also deprived of the ration cards that were indispensable for buying food and other necessary goods.

A final effort to protect the Italians of Zara was made in March 1944 by some officers of the Tenth, who carried out a propaganda mission in the area with the aim of enlisting volunteers. In spite of the extremely difficult circumstances, this mission enjoyed some success. A large number of Italians answered the call. Believing this to be their final stand, even adolescents ran to enlist, including thirteen-year-old Sergio Endrigo, later to become a famous singer. The D'Annunzio Company, charged with the defence of this uttermost part of Italy, was to be almost completely slaughtered by Tito's partisans.

Pavolini Is Treated Like 'the Least of the Albanian Ministers'

The events in Venezia Giulia distressed Mussolini, who had to watch helplessly the denationalization of those lands, which had cost 600,000 Italian lives and on which rested a large part of Fascist rhetoric. All his efforts to regain the Italian provinces incorporated into the Adriatisches Küstenland had come to naught. His efforts to send financial help to Italians in Dalmatia had failed, and so had his plan to send the hospital ships *Italia* and *Gradisca* to Zara to carry its Italians to Italy. The Germans, who used those ships to transport salt, refused his request for the loan of them.

In January 1945, in order to send at least a message of solidarity to Italians in the annexed territories, Mussolini sent the Secretary of the Fascist Republican Party, Alessandro Pavolini, to the Littoral. It would be a voyage full of rage and humiliation.

Pavolini visited Udine and the valleys of the Natisone River, where the guerrilla war was raging. Then he went to Gorizia and carried on to Trieste, Pola, and Fiume. The Duce's envoy met with difficulties and suspicion everywhere he went. The German authorities made it clear to him that he was unwanted. In Pola, they even stopped him at the city gates and, for cooked up reasons, forbade him entrance. In Fiume, the *marò* of the Tenth who escorted him nearly opened fire on the Germans. After paying his respects at the chapel in the cemetery of Cossala to those who had fallen for Fiume, Pavolini was allowed to call upon the provincial secretaries of the Fascist Party of Venezia Giulia. There he heard a general lament against the torments the Germans and the Ustachi were inflicting on the Italians. The situation grew worse in Trieste. Rainer refused to receive him as an Italian minister, but only as secretary of the party, so the meeting was called off. Later, Pavolini was invited to a lunch in his honour offered by a certain Rogalski as a representative of the Supreme Commissariat. When he arrived, he discovered that he was the only Italian present; he also learned that the lunch was being offered by 'comrade' Rogalski to 'comrade' Pavolini. Nothing official, in other words. Offended, Pavolini left the room in protest, while those who stayed behind rejoiced in having treated him 'like the least of the Albanian ministers.'

Pavolini later vented his wrath at the Teatro Verdi to a full audience of Italians. He screamed: 'Sometime, in this advanced trench of ours that is Trieste, at the extreme end of long roads isolated by aerial bombings, because of scarce communications, and because of reasons you know very well, you might have thought that you were far from the Motherland. Well then, I can say only one thing to you: no one more than you, Triestinians and people of Venezia Giulia, is closer to Mussolini's heart.'

His words were met with loud cries in praise of Italy. From the gallery there were cries of 'Long live Italy! Down with the Adriatic Littoral!' The Germans were insulted by this demonstration and, as a sign of protest, cancelled all other meetings set for Pavolini, who could do nothing except return to Salò in a fury and disappointed. His dejected report to Mussolini closed with these bitter words: 'Unfortunately, the torch is going out.'

A Difficult Choice

It was not easy for an Italian to become a partisan in Venezia Giulia. This is another aspect of the tragedy of Venezia Giulia. Elsewhere, a youth who wanted to flee the Fascists and the Nazis could take refuge in the partisan formations that were forming spontaneously in the mountains of the peninsula; in the Littoral, this choice did not exist. Enrolling in Tito's partisan bands meant subjecting oneself to another powerful enemy of Italy. That is why, except for the deluded who believed in the brotherhood of all people, or the Communist militants accustomed to obeying Moscow's directives blindly, no young Italian could become a partisan in Venezia Giulia.

In other parts of Yugoslavia, the situation was different and a number of Italians were members of the occupation forces. For the Alpini from Piedmont or the infantrymen from Sicily who after 8 September had been abandoned to their fate by the High Command, the change meant only a change of front. The new enemies were the Germans, who were slaughtering Italian officers and shipping Italian soldiers to internment camps in Germany or Poland.

Because they were tired, or through personal conviction, or for opportunistic reasons, many Italian soldiers surrendered their weapons to Tito's squads and volunteered to help them fight the Nazis. In Spalato, two hundred Carabinieri and about a hundred soldiers from other units refused to surrender to the Germans; instead, they joined the partisans and created the battalion 'Garibaldi.' Joining up with the battalion 'Matteotti,' which had formed spontaneously in Bosnia, these two groups constituted the 'Italia' brigade. In Montenegro, after bloody encounters with the Germans and the Chetniks, the 'Venezia' and 'Taurinense' divisions, 16,000 men strong, merged with the partisan brigade 'Garibaldi.' However, the Yugoslavs formed only 5,000 Italians into cadres. The others were assigned to other units led by Slavic officers. Later, it became standard practice to break up Italian units and disperse those soldiers among the other partisan formations. By the end of the conflict, there were no autonomous Italian formations anywhere on Yugoslav territory.

The political motives of the Yugoslavs are rather clear today: they wanted absolute control over the guerrilla war, so that they would not owe the Italians anything after the war. At the time, however, these motives were cleverly disguised by relentless propaganda that focused on the common fight against Fascism and on the brotherhood of the people. This propaganda deceived many Italians, who ended up sacrificing themselves for Yugoslavia's war of liberation. Of the 40,000 Italians who participated in that struggle, 20,000 never returned.

In Venezia Giulia, we already noted, the situation was different. Slovenian and Croatian bands had invaded Istria immediately after 8 September, and proceeded to terrorize all Italians, Fascist and non-Fascist alike, to the point that many of them greeted the returning Germans as liberators when the latter launched their counteroffensive. But then the Germans, too, revealed their true nature, and the national question, which had never been resolved, was asked again in a highly dramatic way.

It was the cruelty of the invaders, and not ideological conviction, that led many Istrians to side with the republican Fascism that was starting to rise in the region. In the end, it was the Fascist soldiers – especially the *marò* of the Tenth – who represented the only force willing to fight to defend the Italianness of that territory, which was craved by both the Germans and the Slavs.

The decision to enrol in the partisan bands was not easy for any Italian, whether he was driven by socialist ideals or, more naively, by a belief that this was the path to freedom and democracy. Gaetano La Perna, who himself faced this decision, notes that no group caught in this scenario achieved its goals. Those who joined the Fascists had to consider the possibility that they would become part of the Third Reich if the Germans won. At the same time, the Communists, Socialists, and Democrats well understood that by joining the partisans they were making themselves instruments of Slavic nationalism. History's judgment of the Italians' behaviour in Venezia Giulia cannot ignore this.

The first Italian armed group to take part in the resistance was the Triestinian Proletarian Brigade. The name reveals its ideological stance. It was composed, in fact, of Communist workers and students from Trieste and Monfalcone, and it was led by Vinicio Fontanot, scion of a heroic working-class family from the Monfalcone area, which would sacrifice many of its sons to the liberation struggle.

Often engaged in bloody fighting with the Germans, often decimated and just as often reconstituted, the Proletarian was forced, in the end, to subject itself to the will of the Yugoslav People's Liberation Army. Pushed in that direction by the clandestine Italian Communist Party, it placed itself under the direct control of the Slovenian IX Korpus. To differentiate itself from the other formations, the Proletarian was allowed to use the Italian tricolour with a red star in the centre. This flag would later become the symbol of the Italian minority in Yugoslavia.

Italian Partisans Shot by the *Titini*

Other formations of Italian Communists met a worse fate. The Slavs did not hesitate to kill those who refused to subject themselves to their control. That is what happened, for example, to the Battalion Giovanni Zol, which dared to claim they received their orders only from the Triestinian federation of the Italian Communist Party. Accused of 'insubordination' in front of the Supreme Yugoslav Command, three members of the battalion – Giovanni Pezza, Umberto Dorino, and Mario Zezza – were summarily sentenced to death. Pezza and Dorino were shot immediately; Zezza was able to save himself. Still more tragic was the fate of Captain Filippo Casini of the Carabinieri. A thirty-year-old Genoese, recently married, Casini was not at all a Communist; however, contact with members of the Resistance had convinced him that the common struggle against the German oppressor could help save the Italian soul of the Istria he loved so deeply.

On 2 July 1944, in his capacity as commander of the Carabinieri Group of Pola, Captain Casini transferred himself and the more than one hundred men under his command to the partisans. A few days later, he was joined by his bride Luciana, a young woman from Pola who wanted to follow her husband's destiny. It would be a horrible destiny. Very soon after, the Yugoslavs made it known that whoever fought alongside them would have to share their annexationist goals. Naturally, the captain did not accept this, so the Yugoslavs quickly handed him over to a People's Tribunal, which sentenced him to death, together with his wife Luciana, who wanted to remain at his side. Both of them were shot on 14 August 1944, a little over a month after joining the partisans.

The Carabinieri who had followed Captain Casini were dispersed among the various units and deployed far from Istria. Their fate is unknown. Captain Filippo Casini was posthumously awarded the Gold Medal for Military Valour.

The Einheit 'R' Enters on Scene

Intense guerrilla activity in the mountains and plateaux of the Adriatic Littoral did not prevent the Germans from carrying out their 'Final

Solution to the Jewish problem' in the new province of the Reich. In October 1943, soon after the founding of the Adriatisches Küstenland, SS Gruppenführer Odilo Globocnik established in Trieste the Einheit 'R,' a special unit of 'Jew hunters.' It consisted of veterans of Treblinka who had already worked for him. There were about one hundred of them; most were Ukrainian and still wore the uniform of the Red Army. Under the command of commissioned and non-commissioned SS officers, their assignment was 'to set up the necessary measures that would later be put into action for the elimination of Jews.' These measures, as one can easily guess, included identifying and capturing Jews and sequestering their goods and real estate. The Einheit 'R' later set up detachments in Fiume, Udine, and Castelnuovo d'Istria. In Trieste, its headquarters were at the *risiera* of San Sabba, an old, dark, cavernous building that had once been used for drying raw rice. The Germans now converted it into a detention centre.

As soon as Globonik took over command of the regional police, he dissolved the Council of the Jewish Community and closed down the synagogue. He noted at the time that most of his 'prey' had already escaped. Before the war, there had been five thousand Jews in Trieste. The more prominent families in that community had emigrated before the war started. Many of those who remained had blended with other groups, often taking refuge with friends or in areas of the countryside considered less dangerous. The Jews who had been interned under the Fascist regime had taken advantage of the confusion that followed the fall of Mussolini, fleeing the camps to seek refuge elsewhere, often in Switzerland. Those who remained, most of them elderly or destitute, had tried to assume new identities, perhaps by having themselves baptized. In the end, this would not save them from arrest and deportation.

According to historian Pier Arrigo Carnier, the men of the Einheit 'R' captured about three hundred Jews, who were detained in the *risiera* before being deported to the castle of Hartheim, near Linz, in Austria. There, they were gassed and then burnt in crematoria. However, other historians contend that many Jews were killed and gassed in the *risiera* itself, which today has been identified as the only extermination camp that the Nazis operated in Italy. We will have reason to return to this controversial episode.

This Jew hunting was lucrative for the Nazis, who began by sequestering several splendid villas in Trieste belonging to wealthy Jews who had emigrated and turning them into residences for high officials. They then began carrying away from them everything of value: antiques, paintings by renowned artists, entire art collections, and all sorts of precious objects. Part of this booty went to Germany to adorn the houses of the Nazi leaders. The rest was discovered after the war in the warehouses in the port. Also, around fifteen businesses belonging to Jewish families were sequestered and liquidated. The revenues were appropriated by the government of the Littoral.

'Dr Manzoni,' Hunter of Jews

The man who helped the Nazis capture the last Jews of Trieste was named Negri (his first name is not known), and was himself a renegade Jew who hid his true identity behind the appearance of a distinguished gentleman. He was of Polish extraction; his family had moved from Galicia to Trieste when the city was still part of the Hapsburg Empire. His original surname was Schwarz, but under the Fascists, it had been translated into Negri.

Negri, who preferred to present himself as 'Dr Manzoni,' had made contact with the SS command right after 8 September and had asked to be enrolled in the secret service. As credentials, he provided the Nazis with the names and addresses of 180 Jewish families in Trieste. Later, after he had been awarded officer's rank, he himself would be assigned to arrest them. This despicable man worked in tandem with his mistress, a thirty-something Triestinian woman whose name is not known, and received from the Nazis a bounty for every captured Jew. Even Negri's father, an old Galician tailor, participated in the enterprise: his son set him up inside the *risiera* as director of the sewing shop, where the detainees were put to work making uniforms for German soldiers.

After he had finished scouring the littoral for Jews, the Germans assigned 'Dr Manzoni' to secret missions in Duce-Italien, their name for the Italian Social Republic. He worked in Milan, Padua, Venice, and other cities raking in dozens of Jews, nearly all of them over seventy, thus violating the weak laws of the Social Republic according to which the elderly could not be imprisoned. The diabolical couple often took advantage of their position to extort money from those unfortunates who fell into their hands.

Like the notorious 'General Della Rovere,' whose deeds Indro Montanelli recounted in his book, which Roberto Rossellini transformed into a movie starring Vittorio De Sica, so, too, 'Dr Manzoni' was in the habit of going to the houses of those whom he had arrested to extort money in exchange for false promises of release. In Venice, his mistress obtained some precious objects from a young Jewish woman who was about to give birth, on the promise she would save her and the newborn from arrest. They were both, instead, arrested and deported to places unknown.

The criminal activities of 'Dr Manzoni' lasted almost to the end of the war. In the end, the Germans themselves were scandalized by his ignoble behaviour. His downfall came about in the dramatic days when the Germans were evacuating Trieste under threat from Tito's armies. His superiors sentenced him to death on the rather curious accusation that he had violated the laws of the Italian Social Republic – laws that forbade the arrest of Jews over the age of seventy. The truth is that he and his mistress had become dangerous witnesses and, for this reason, had to be eliminated. Negri was killed in the Gestapo manner, with a revolver shot to the head. His mistress was strangled by a Ukrainian auxiliary. Their bodies were burned in the *risiera*.

The *Risiera* 'versus' the *Foibe*

Was San Sabba really the only Nazi extermination camp to operate in Italy? Clearly not, if we adhere to the horrible and apocalyptic meaning that term has acquired in collective memory. The *risiera*, in fact, never operated as an extermination camp. We do not wish, however, to start counting the dead or to join those who, with complicated as well as useless calculations, try to prove that the victims of the Holocaust were not six million, but five or four – as if a hundred, a thousand, or a million fewer deaths could attenuate the responsibility of the Nazi butchers in the face of history. What we are seeking, instead, is to dispel some of the confusion that for more than half a century has surrounded the macabre competition between *foibe* and *risiera*, between those who seek to link these two and those who would rather distinguish them.

In the Adriatic Littoral, the Germans behaved as brutally as they did in every other territory they occupied. The Italians in the cities and towns occupied by the *Titini* had greeted the Germans as liberators, but soon learned that they were even worse than the partisans. A long nightmare began marked by raids, roundups, assaults, and bloody reprisals. There were countless summary executions and public hangings. In Opicina, after a bomb exploded in a cinema, seventy Italian and Slovenian hostages were shot; their bodies were then tossed into a *foiba* in the Carso. In Trieste, after a bombing at the Soldatenheim, the Soldiers' House, fifty-one Triestinians were hung along via Ghega and left in public view for days. Other public executions were carried out on via Massimo d'Azeglio, in Prosecco, at the gas station in Trieste, and in many other locations. In the meantime, hundreds of Jews, along with Yugoslav and Italian partisans, were detained in the *risiera*. The building had been transformed into a prison camp, complete with sleeping barracks, torture chambers, punishment cells, and other works of the Nazi devil. Most of the guards were Ukrainian and had come from Treblinka, where the Nazis had taught them how to exterminate prisoners with poison gas.

In the *risiera*, however, there were no gas chambers. Nor is there any record that mass exterminations were carried out there. There was, however, a rudimentary crematorium, which the Treblinka veterans had built from an old rice drier. Many bodies were burned in this oven. The Jews held in the *risiera* were deported to extermination camps in Austria and Poland. In the *risiera*, only individual executions were carried out; the bodies were then burned in the adjoining crematorium, which was also used to burn the bodies of prisoners who had died of natural causes or of hostages and partisans shot elsewhere. Records indicate that in the spring of 1944, the bodies of about fifty Yugoslav partisans were trucked in from Istria for cremation in the *risiera*.

Franz Suchomel, an SS officer who worked in Treblinka and then at the *risiera*, declared cooly in his deposition at an Allied tribunal that the oven in the Trieste camp 'did not have good draft'; cremations, he added, 'must be done on a grate so that the draft comes from underneath.' In short, the *risiera* was not Treblinka. The guards did not use fuel, but simply firewood and so, to quote the Nazi jailer once again, 'the bodies of the men did not burn as well as those of the women.'

A brief picture of life inside the Trieste lager can be drawn from the written account by Bruno Piazza, an Italian partisan who survived deportation:

> The *risiera* of San Sabba, a large building with enormous halls with wooden ceilings, with attached crematorium that the Germans used to burn their victims, had been set up by the SS as an antechamber in which to gather the victims destined for the extermination camps in Germany ... In the week I have been here I have heard them kill thirty persons, all partisans. Rhythmic steps in the courtyard. Pistol shots. Dogs howling. Silence ... In spite of it all, being in the *risiera* was preferable to being deported. Here, at

least, we were still in our own country ... My transfer, I found out later, had enormous importance. It was a measure that was later to save my life and save me from the gas chamber and the crematorium. I was transferred, in fact, from the category of racial detainee to that of political detainee and, while for the former, if over fifty years of age, there was the crematorium the moment one arrived at the camp, for the latter, whether or not one was fit, there was the labour camp, and not the gas chamber and the oven ... The Jews of the *risiera*, about eighty men, women, and children, are locked in two wagons behind ours. Among them I recognized Dr Vivante and Mr Elio Mordo, whom I had left in the *risiera* the previous day ... Unlike ours, the two wagons containing the eighty Jews from the *risiera* are still shut.

Immediately after the war, popular opinion spread the view that the *risiera* had been an extermination camp like Treblinka, Auschwitz, and Mauthausen. This rumour was not supported at the trial of Rainer, conducted in Ljubljana by the Yugoslav Military Tribunal. (The accused would be sentenced to death. His trial took place in July 1947, and was held in Ljubljana because at that time Trieste was considered by the Yugoslavs to be part of Slovenia, whose capital was Ljubljana.) In all of the many accusations levelled against Rainer, there is no mention of an 'extermination camp' in the *risiera*. On the contrary, the sentence states that captured partisans and political prisoners from the Adriatic Littoral were deported to the death camps of Dachau, Auschwitz, and Mauthausen. My point is that the question of whether the *risiera* was an extermination camp or merely a transit camp toward extermination is of no real importance. What is important is how this question was later exploited for political purposes.

The painful dispute exploded in the press in 1975 on the occasion of the thirtieth anniversary of the Liberation. Up until that time, Italians knew little or nothing about the *foibe*, much less about the *risiera*. The topic was taboo, or as we now say, politically incorrect. No one spoke of the *foibe*, not even in textbooks (and unfortunately, we have continued not to speak of them). The memory of the victims had been kept alive only in the restricted circles of the Julian diaspora, and only thanks to the work of the Association of the Fallen without a Cross (Associazione Caduti senza Croce). Even commemorative ceremonies were restricted to the religious sphere and were usually promoted by Monsignor Antonio Santin, the heroic bishop of Trieste, who in the difficult years of the war had confronted with equal courage the Germans, the Fascists, and the Communists. Italian government officials were never present at these commemorations.

Some years later, the Italian government declared the *risiera* a 'national monument,' on par with the Fosse Ardeatine, pointing out that this was 'the only Nazi extermination camp to operate in Italy.' The proposals advanced by the Julian associations to commemorate the *foibe* of Basovizza and Monrupino – the only ones left on Italian national territory after the new borders were drawn – fell on deaf ears.

The debate between the two sides flared up again later. On the one side were those who insisted that the *foibe*, 'a place of pain and anguish,' had to be seen as on par with the *risiera* and the Fosse Ardeatine 'because a crime committed by the loser or by the winner remains always a crime.' On the other side were those who maintained that the slaughters in the *risiera* could not be compared with those at the *foibe* because the former were part of a planned genocide, whereas the latter were the unleashing of 'a spiral of reciprocal and ancient provocations among opposing nationalities.'

We now come to 25 April 1975. On the occasion of the thirtieth anniversary of the Liberation, the President of Italy, Giovanni Leone, arrived in Trieste. On that occasion, too, the *foibe* were ignored. The ceremony took place in the courtyard of the *risiera* where, in the presence of the President of Italy, the official commemoration address was given by a Slovenian in Slovenian and thus was not understood by most of the people present. This episode of debatable taste, to say the least, did not fail to raise murmurs of protest.

Perhaps to make up for the gaffe, perhaps in a spontaneous gesture, the following day President Leone had a laurel wreath bearing the insignia of the President of the Republic placed in front of the memorial stone at Basovizza. This gesture softened the protests of the Triestinians but was loudly condemned by the Yugoslavs. In an angry note from the official agency 'Tanjug,' the Italian head of state was accused of having given in to pressure from neo-Fascists and right-wing parties and of having 'clouded the ceremonies for the thirtieth anniversary of the Liberation' by honouring 'a monument dedicated to Nazis and Fascists.' A few hours later, the president's wreath was taken away by Slavic hoodlums and burned.

The *risiera–foibe* debate continued to churn up controversy, and not just among Triestinians. To avoid irritating 'friendly' Yugoslavia, and to avoid conflicts within the 'constitutional spectrum,' the government opted to play down the *foibe* and to play up the *risiera*. This obviously left in the hands of the neo-Fascists (and of course, in the hands of the families of the victims of the *foibe*) the duty of preserving the memory of the thousands of Italians who today must be seen as the first victims of modern ethnic cleansing in what is now ex-Yugoslavia.

The conviction that the *foibe* are 'full of Fascists' has sunk deep roots in Italy's collective imaginary. Even prestigious publications have committed this error; for example, in June 1982 the weekly magazine *Panorama* raised a storm of protest when it simplistically defined the *foiba* of Basovizza as a 'great tomb of Fascists.'

The subject of the *foibe* has long been considered an awkward topic. This can be seen in the convoluted way in which it was granted official recognition on 12 June 1982, on the thirty-seventh anniversary of the liberation of Trieste from the Yugoslavs. On that day, a decree from the Ministry of Natural Resources, then headed by Giovanni Spadolini, declared the *foibe* of Basovizza and Monrupino not 'national monuments' but 'monuments of national interest,' with the following ambiguous rationale: 'Testimony of tragic events at the end of the Second World War; mass graves for a noteworthy number of civil and military victims, for the most part Italians, killed and thrown in them.'

Giovanni Spadolini was supposed to be present at the ceremony at the *foiba* of Basovizza, but at the last moment a pressing commitment kept him in Rome. He was represented by the Undersecretary for Industry, Senator Rebecchini. Roberto Spazzali, who wrote a long book about this awkward incident, notes that the low-key celebration of the event was commented on bitterly in the local press. One newspaper pointed out that the previous year, the Italian president, Sandro Pertini, on an official visit to Trieste, had paid his respects to the *risiera* but had 'forgotten' Basovizza: 'There was no bugler or band, not a military guard to pay its respects to the many soldiers who lay at the bottom of the chasm. There is no indication that any message was received from the President's Office or from the Prime Minister's Office.'

The large crowd in attendance criticized the complete silence of the minor government representative. And it openly contested the speech of the official speaker, the Honourable Paolo Barbi, who, as the newspapers reported, 'had paired off the thousands of victims of the *foibe* with the martyrs of the Fosse Ardeatine, forgetting that the man responsible for the latter crime has been serving his sentence in jail for many years, while those responsible for the *foibe* have been decorated with medals by the Republic of Italy.' Here, the journalist was referring to SS Colonel Herbert Kappler, who at that time was serving his sentence in Gaeta.

Many years later, the debate was reignited when the Italian Justice Department arranged the extradition from Argentina of SS Captain Erich Priebke, an old collaborator of Kappler. The newspapers of the Julian exiles asked in vain for a similar extradition for the 'Yugoslav Priebkes' – that is, for the 'butcher of Pisino,' Ivan Motika, for the Croatian Oskar Piskulic, and for many others still alive who had been responsible for the *foibe* and against whom a similar albeit late-incoming judicial process had been started.

Two scales and two measures? Absolutely. As we have already said, historians have nearly always kept quiet about or skipped over the *foibe*, even in school textbooks. The most disturbing example is found in the most widely available Italian encyclopaedia, the *Garzantina*. When you look under F for 'Fosse Ardeatine,' you find a succinct but very clear explanation of that horrendous massacre carried out by the Nazis on 24 March 1944 at the sandpits near the catacombs of San Callisto in Rome. But when you read the entry for *'foibe,'* you find: 'A type of sink-hole found in Istria.' That's all.

Only for the sixth edition of the encyclopaedia, dated 1998, was the following statement added: 'Between 1943 and 1945 they were the site of massacres of Italians (from 5,000 to 10,000, according to estimates) carried out by the partisan troops of Marshal Tito.' Better late than never.

Italians Alone against Everybody

Foibe or *risiera, risiera* or *foibe*. Very simplistically, towards the end of 1944, for Italians in Venezia Giulia there was no choice. Alone against everyone, frightened and disoriented, with the prospect only of passing from the watchful and rational oppression of the Germans to the brutal and irrational oppression of the Slavs, they no longer knew, in the true sense of the word, which saint to pray to. The only glimmer of hope, an Anglo-American landing in the northern Adriatic that had been much talked about in those last few months, had definitely disappeared. The Allies, in fact, had chosen to land in southern France so as not to upset Stalin, who did not want intruders in that part of Europe which he already assumed to be his sphere of influence.

As a result, there was no way out for Italians. The few armed units of the Italian Social Republic still present in the territory offered only faint protection. They were only a few hundred men, and except for the Tenth Mas, they were so much under the thumb of the Germans that

Italo Sauro, one of the sons of the hero who fought in vain to defend the Italianness of the region, established an underground anti-Slav and anti-German newspaper, which was then distributed in Istria, with great difficulty. Then there were the Slavs: the Ustachi, Chetniks, and Domobranci, who enjoyed the protection of the Germans; and the *Titini* partisans, who enjoyed the backing of the Allies. Both sides were united in their hatred for Italians and in their common goal of conquering and annexing, once the war was over, the entire region of Venezia Giulia up to and beyond the Tagliamento River.

Even among the most fervent Italian Communists, those who had obeyed the instructions of the party and joined the Yugoslav partisans, the first concerns did not take long to appear. The leaders of the Garibaldi-Natisone Division, the strongest Italian formation in the area, which had passed under the command of the Slovenian IX Korpus, reported to the underground headquarters of the Italian Communist Party that the Italians and the Slavs were disagreeing violently every time the region's future was raised for discussion. 'One sees too many Yugoslav flags around and few red flags,' the old militants of the Third International commented. Whenever they heard the word 'Motherland,' Slavic or Italian as she might be, their hair stood on end.

The less fervent Italian Communists, the ones more inclined to go along, were alarmed by the partisans' forceful propaganda, which struck fear among Italians by declaring that, with Stalin's help, Yugoslavia was going to get Trieste, Pola, Fiume, and Zara, and that the treatment the Italians received from their new country would depend on their behaviour.

For its part, the Italian Communist Party openly embraced the Yugoslav line. In a directive penned by Mauro Scoccimarro, at that time a member of the government of the South, we read: 'Before the arrival of the Allies, Venezia Giulia must be conquered by the Yugoslav partisans and by the Italian partisans fighting alongside them ... For all intents and purposes, Italian partisans fighting with the Yugoslav formations must be considered Yugoslav partisans ... In Venezia Giulia the only patriots are those fighting alongside the Yugoslavs.'

Thanks to its leading role in the Italian Resistance, the Italian Communist Party was able to get the National Liberation Committee for Northern Italy to send the following invitation to the Julian people, although it was aware that the Communists had abandoned the National Liberation Committee of Trieste: 'Create Italo-Slovenian and Italo-Croatian anti-Fascist committees that, besides organizing the struggle against the common oppressor, will also have the goal of harmonizing the interest of the two people. Your duty is to enlist in the Italian units fighting in your region under the command of Marshal Tito in the common liberation war. The armies of Marshal Tito are part of the great armies of the United Nations: you will fight at their side as at the side of liberating brothers.' In a surge of 'solidarity,' the National Liberation Committee for Northern Italy loaned Tito's partisans three million lire (half the capital at its disposal), which would never be repaid and which would never pay, either, any political returns.

The Government of the South and the 'Julian Case'

By early 1945, it was clear who was going to win the war, and the Italian government of the South, headquartered in Salerno, was growing more and more concerned about the tragedy taking shape in Venezia Giulia. Knowing the expansionist designs of Tito, and fearing a repeat of the atrocities of October 1943, the Italian leaders had tried to reach an agreement directly with the Yugoslavs. When that effort failed, they sought to reach an understanding with the Allies so that when the Germans finally surrendered, they would occupy the region and thus prevent or limit the inevitable Yugoslav reprisals. The news from Trieste was bleak. An unsigned memo discovered by Paola Romano reads in part:

> It is possible that the acts of violence and radical eradication carried out at times by the valiant Yugoslav partisans might recently have changed and that in place of previous practice, which has taken place with terrible consequences mainly in Istria, more humane directives and discipline might have been introduced. But one should consider the danger that, justifying the means with the end, a vast slaughter may be perpetrated, as precedent leads us to fear, and that there may be, in part, a moral and political compression of the Italian population.

A distressing forecast, but confirmed on all points. On the other hand, the Italian Government of the South could do very little for the Julians. Considering that Italy was a defeated country, the Allies would never have allowed that government to interfere in their military operations. Its timid attempt to reach an understanding was ignored, and the Allies refused even to let it know their intentions for the region. Britain's General Harold Alexander, commander of the Allied forces in Italy, had refused to allow units of the Italian Army of the South to go defend Venezia Giulia.

Regarding the Julian question, the three victorious powers had taken conflicting positions even before the war's end. The Soviet Union obviously favoured Tito; Stalin, underestimating the partisan leader's character and political acumen, already saw Yugoslavia as a future satellite of Moscow. The United States favoured Italy because it bore no illusions about the advance of Communism in Yugoslavia. The Americans wanted no part of any 'Balkan complications,' but they hoped to make Italy a bastion against Soviet expansionism and Trieste the head of its supply lines for the U.S. Army in central Europe.

The British position was different. At that time, London still followed an imperialist politic and the Mediterranean was part of its interests. It also hoped to keep alive the Churchill–Stalin accord signed in Moscow in October 1944, according to which the two countries would exercise an equal influence over Yugoslavia.

So much for the political level. However, one must not forget – as some historians have done when they have criticized Britain's harshness toward Italy – that Great Britain owed Yugoslavia a moral debt. Winston Churchill could not forget the promises he had made in 1941 from his besieged island to the Yugoslav partisans, who were the first to rise up against the Germans, then lords of Europe. It is true that Churchill had made these promises to General Mihajlović, but it is also true that he afterwards abandoned the Chetniks in order to support Tito ('one of the greatest mistakes of the Second World War,' Churchill himself would admit in his memoirs). As a result, Tito considered himself the legitimate recipient of the British 'cheque.' Furthermore, one could not deny that his partisans had contributed greatly to the victory over Nazism. In the collective imagination of the British, Italy was a former enemy. Mussolini had at one point asked Hitler for 'the honour to send his own planes to bomb London,' and his country had for three years fought strongly against the British Army. These things must be remembered when the behaviour of the British in Trieste seems especially odious.

So in the last months of the war, Tito was in a strong position with respect to Italy. He could boast about his success against the common enemy, he could count on Stalin's total support, and he could show General Alexander's signature at the bottom of a secret Yugo-British accord whereby, after Venezia Giulia was occupied, and pending the redrawing of national borders, Yugoslavia would be assigned the civilian administration of Trieste.

In the Kingdom of the South, the Allies' disinterest in the Julian question was noted, so the next step was somehow to contact the less fanatical elements of the Italian Social Republic and lay out a common front aimed at preserving the Julian region for Italy. Without informing the Allies or the Communist elements in the government – which would certainly have killed at birth any moves in this direction – the South sent several envoys to the North to contact the more approachable elements of the Social Republic, but nearly all these missions failed. When not faint-hearted, the Fascists were simply opportunistic: those who said they were open for a discussion turned out to be more interested in saving their own lives than in national unity.

The only attempt along these lines worth noting was the one by the men of the Tenth Mas. This special unit of the Italian Royal Navy was animated by a strong sense of comradeship, and this made its men natural intermediaries between North and South. The Tenth had been created before 8 September, and under the command of Junio Valerio Borghese had carried out some of the most memorable actions of the Mediterranean war. At Suda, Malta, Alexandria, and Gibraltar, with a handful of men aboard 'pigs' – small explosive boats – they had brought the British Mediterranean Fleet to its knees, sinking more ships than the Italian Royal Navy had managed in the entire war.

On 8 September, the Tenth had been split in two, and now the Northern force was fighting against the Southern one, albeit in a very chivalrous and rather goliardic fashion. For example, the Southern forces would step into the gulf of La Spezia, and having finished their operation slip back out, leaving behind mocking messages for their Northern comrades. And when the *marò* from the North captured a *marò* from the South, they would celebrate the reunion, notwithstanding the civil war that was underway. It is easy to understand, then, why it turned out to be especially easy to establish contacts between the two fronts by taking advantage of friendships that the civil war had not been able to break.

'The Man Who Came from the South'

In March 1945, with the military campaign quickly drawing to a close, the Americans agreed to provide cover for a final attempt to contact the Tenth in the North. The mission was assigned to the Triestinian Antonio Marceglia, a heroic officer who, on 18 December 1941, together with Luigi Durand de la Penne and Vincenzo Martellotta, had entered the port at Alexandria aboard three 'pigs' and sunk the battleship *Queen Elizabeth* (while de la Penne sank the battleship *Valiant* and Martellotta a large oil tanker). After this exploit, for which he received a Gold Medal, Marceglia was captured by the British and deported to India. After the Italian armistice, he received permission to return to service with the Tenth of the South.

As soon as Marceglia re-entered service, he and some other Julians founded in Taranto a patriotic association called Lega Adriatica, whose aim, besides providing assistance to Julian soldiers and civilians scattered throughout the Italy of the South, was to keep national ties strong and to select capable individuals to send across the border to the North. He hoped to create in Venezia Giulia a number of Italian resistance groups and to develop a single national front to fight both the Germans and the Slavs. The aim of his new mission, for which he had volunteered, was to contact at La Spezia his old commander, Junio Valerio Borghese, and induce him to join his men in a united front for the defence of the region.

On the evening of 27 March 1945, Marceglia came out of an American submarine near the coast and, aboard a rubber dinghy, reached the beach at Marina di Carrara. But the Germans were waiting for him here. Captured and taken to the jail in La Spezia, 'the man who came from the South' was able, thanks to the complicity of an Italian prison guard, to send a note to the commander of the Tenth in the nearby barracks of San Bartolomeo. The message consisted of only two words – *Sono prigioniero* (I am captured) – and his signature.

The camaraderie that held together the men of the Tenth sprang immediately into action: the commander, Mario Arillo, also a Gold Medal recipient for his deeds at Gibraltar, obtained his immediate release. The following day, wearing the uniform of an officer of the Tenth of the North, Marceglia met Captain Borghese in Venice. He quickly realized that the situation had become desperate. Borghese told him that contacts had been established with the Osoppo Brigade, the only autonomous Italian formation still operating in the area, but that they had been interrupted for reasons of *force majeure*, which we will later have an opportunity to examine. The other partisan formations contacted by Marceglia proved to be deaf to his appeals for unity, and the National Liberation Committee in Trieste seemed to him inefficient, if not 'a phantom and non-existent.' Here is a passage from the memo Marceglia drafted at the end of his mission:

Borghese told me he sent his units in Venezia Giulia to protect this region from German and Slavic designs. Some days later he led me to Lonato where he affirmed that I could inform the government of the South of his agreement on the matters discussed. He did not want to make a common front with those of the South but, from the point of view of national interest, he was in agreement. He gave me a pass and I went to Trieste where I realized that the National Liberation Committee did not have sufficient forces to act at the opportune moment against the Slavs and the Germans. Then I moved to Venice where I saw Borghese again who told me his plan, which consisted of proposing to Mussolini the formation of a single front for the defence of Trieste. This, however, could not be carried out because events rushed ahead.

In other words, the mission had been a complete failure. By now, the death knell was ringing for Venezia Giulia. The government of the South was helpless, and some were resigned or favourable to ceding the entire region to Yugoslavia. At the same time, a violent pro-Tito campaign was being carried out that denied the existence of the *foibe* and that accused anyone who raised the Julian question, or who urged members of the Resistance to defend Trieste and Istria, of being a Fascist provocateur.

A threatening letter addressed to Prime Minister Ivanoe Bonomi by Palmiro Togliatti, founder and secretary of the Italian Communist Party, is highly revealing on this matter. This letter, discovered in the archives by the Istrian historian Antonio Pitamitz, is dated 7 February 1945 and reads:

I was told that on behalf of our colleague Gasparotto a communication has been sent to the National Liberation Committee for Northern Italy inviting the Committee to see to it that our partisan units take Venezia Giulia under their control so as to prevent units of the Yugoslav partisan army from penetrating in it. I would hope this is not true because, first of all, instruction of this kind could not have been issued without consulting the Council of Ministers. As for the internal situation, this is a directive of civil war, because it is absurd to think that our party would accept to engage in a struggle against the anti-Fascist and democratic forces of Tito. On this line, furthermore, our organization in Trieste has had precise instructions from me personally and the majority of the people of Trieste today follows our party. Not only do we not want any conflict with Tito's forces and with the Yugoslav population, but we believe that the only instruction to be given is for our partisan units and for the Italians of Trieste and Venezia Giulia to collaborate in the strictest sense with Tito's units in the struggle against the Germans and against the Fascists.

The Slaughter at Porzus

In the Italian Resistance, the Communist component (which was the majority) always behaved loyally toward fellow combatants of different political beliefs. Clashes or disagreements between 'reds' and 'whites' are isolated and striking exceptions. Absolute solidarity and brotherhood in the armed struggle against the common enemy was the rule. In Venezia Giulia, in contrast, because of the unique circumstances and the overwhelming Slavic presence, the 'red' and 'white' partisans found it difficult to get along, and this led to incidents of great savagery.

Besides the Slovenian IX Korpus, strong in men and supplies, there were two Italian divisions in the area: the Garibaldi-Natisone Division, which had clear Communist leanings; and the Osoppo Division, most of whom were Alpini and wore tricolour neckerchiefs as clear evidence of their patriotism. Differences between the two formations did not take long to flare up: the Communists saw the 'whites' of the Osoppo as no better than the Chetniks and the Domobranci, and obstructed them in every way possible. The situation came to a sudden head when the Italian partisans received the order from the Italian Communist Party to place themselves under the command of the Slovenian IX Korpus. This was on 22 November 1944. A few days earlier, Palmiro Togliatti, secretary of the Italian Communist Party, had written to Vincenzo Bianco ('Colonel Krieger'), the party's representative in the Slovenian IX Korpus, explaining why this order had been issued: 'We consider the occupation of the Julian region by the troops of Marshal Tito a positive fact that should make us happy and that we must support in every way. This means that in this region there will be no English occupation nor a restoration of the reactionary Italian administration, that is, a profoundly different situation from what exists in the free part of Italy will be created. In short, a democratic situation will be created.'

The order to integrate with the army of Marshal Tito was ill received by the Garibaldi-Natisone partisans, but after the intervention of Bianco himself and of the leaders of the Friulian branch of the Italian Communist Party, the 3,500 men of that division decided 'enthusiastically' to transfer the command of the Slovenian IX Korpus. The same order was disdainfully rejected by the partisans of the Osoppo Brigade. Their leader, the young Alpini captain Francesco De Gregori, a Roman and the uncle of the famous singer by the same name, declared frankly to the Communist envoys that his men would not replace their tricolour neckerchief with the red ones of the Slavic partisans.

The popular, anti-Communist version of the Porzus massacre attributes the death of Captain De Gregori and his companions to this patriotic choice, but it is likely there were other reasons besides. The Slavic spies who had infiltrated the Italian unit could not have missed the attempts that envoys of the Tenth Mas were making to establish a dialogue with the Osoppo with the goal of creating an anti-Slavic front to defend the territory for Italy. The Osoppo's refusal to join with the Slovenian IX Korpus would then have drawn suspicion toward the Italian partisans. In situations like this, suspicion can ignite an explosion.

A few months passed. In the Communist federation in Udine, now dominated by the Slavs, something dark was brewing. The Osoppo, decimated by a series of mop-up campaigns, established its headquarters in the woods of Porzus, outside Udine. Its leader, 'Bolla' (the battle name of Francesco De Gregori), was engaged with his closest aides – Gastone Valente ('Enea'), Giovanni Comin ('Gruaro'), and others – in reconstructing the unit. A new recruit had recently joined the group – twenty-year-old Guido Pasolini, brother of the future writer and movie director Pier Paolo Pasolini. There was also a girl, Elda Turchetti, whom the Communists would later finger as a spy of the Tenth Mas. More likely, she was simply an intermediary entrusted with establishing contacts between the Osoppo and the Tenth for the purpose of developing the common Italian front alluded to earlier.

On the morning of 7 February 1945, the guards spotted a group of armed men climbing the flank of Mount Carnizza in scattered formation. They were partisans from the Garibaldi, with the red star on their berets and a red kerchief around their neck. They were led by the Paduan Mario Toffanin (battle name 'Giacca'). He explained to the guards that he had escaped a roundup and wanted to transfer, with his hundred or so men, into the command of Bolla.

When Bolla was informed of this, he sent Valente to see what was going on. A while later, when Valente did not return, he himself climbed down toward the guard positions. At this point a tragedy unfolded, the details of which are not known. Giacca, who had already disarmed Valente, easily captured Bolla as well; he then ordered his men to shoot them. Their bodies would be found later, disfigured by blows and dagger wounds. Right after this, Giacca ordered his men to hunt down the other 'white' partisans, who by now were trying to escape to the chestnut grove of Bosco Romagno. One after the other, Bolla's men fell into the net, except for one – an Alpini officer named Aldo Bricco, who despite being wounded, saved himself by sprinting down the mountain. There was no escape for the prisoners: they were beaten and spat upon, then cut down by machine-gun fire. Among the twenty-two dead were Elda Turchetti and Guido Pasolini.

In this way unfolded the most disturbing episode of the partisan war in Italy: a fratricidal slaughter that threw a dark shadow on the Friulian resistance.

Since then it has been impossible to shed light on this painful episode. No witnesses survived the slaughter. We know only that Mario Toffanin had fought in Tito's bands since before 8 September 1943. He had arrived in Friuli toward the end of 1944. On 2 February 1945, after making contact with the Communist federation and with Giovanni Padoan ('Vanni'), the political commissar of the Garibaldi-Natisone, he had mysteriously assembled a Garibaldi Battalion, which disbanded, just as mysteriously, a few days after the Porzus massacre.

After the war, thirty-seven perpetrators of the massacre were identified, arrested, and tried in Lucca. Condemned to a total of eight hundred years in jail, they were soon freed in the general amnesty promoted by Palmiro Togliatti. Vanni and Giacca were condemned in absentia to thirty years, but they had already taken refuge in Yugoslavia. Later they moved to Czechoslovakia. Vanni was pardoned in 1959, and Giacca in 1978 by President Pertini. Giacca was even granted, with arrears, a military pension of 670,000 lire per month, which INPS, Italy's national pension plan, continues to send him. Toffanin ('Giacca') still lives in Slovenia, at Skofije (Scoffie), five hundred metres from the Italian border. He has never repudiated his crimes, and he is demanding that the INPS pay him the pension of his deceased wife.

The Race for Trieste

The painful incident at Porzus does not mean that the Italian Resistance in Venezia Giulia was forcefully absorbed by its Yugoslav counterpart. There is no shortage of similar episodes in which sectarianism and chauvinism overcame reason, but in nearly all cases the absorption was voluntary. First, because the thousands of Italian soldiers who joined Tito's formations after 8 September came from outside the Julian context and were ignorant of its complex ethnic divisions. Second, because in the end even the Julian anti-Fascists allowed themselves to be seduced by the heroic legend that now surrounded the victorious Marshal Tito, not to mention by the incessant propaganda that promised, at war's end, a fraternal solution to all problems.

There also was no alternative. Italian political forces were in no position to direct, coordinate, support groups in the field. The Trieste National Liberation Committee had been deserted by its Communist members, who elsewhere constituted the driving force behind resistance organizations. It had thus been reduced to a simple rhetorical figure – a circle of well-mannered gentlemen, Socialists, Catholics, liberals, activists – who could offer no guarantee that the struggle would continue in an autonomous manner. This enabled the leaders of the Slavic Resistance to consolidate their political and military authority over the entire region. The result was that such a delicate area of the Italian national territory came to lack any autonomous Italian presence in the Resistance.

Tito was extremely jealous of his own independence (Yugoslavia, as we know, was the only country in eastern Europe to free itself of the Germans without the help of the Red Army). He had no intention of sharing with anyone the liberation of Venezia Giulia, especially with the Italians. The Italian formations operating within the Slovenian IX Korpus would soon be transferred to other fronts in the interior of Yugoslavia so that it would be clear that Trieste had been liberated exclusively by the Yugoslavs.

The operations that in a matter of a few weeks would bring the Yugoslav forces to occupy the greater part of Venezia Giulia had been preceded by long and complex negotiations between the Allies and representatives of the Yugoslav Resistance. At the time of the armistice of 8 September, the British and Americans were committed to occupying the entire Italian territory 'inside the borders of 1939.' Afterwards, however, although the Americans continued to strongly favour Italy or, as an alternative, the creation of a Free State of Trieste under the guiding hand of an Allied military government, the English did not hesitate to express an open mind regarding Yugoslavian territorial requests.

Tito knew very well how to profit from the British stance. Not surprisingly, in later years he would pride himself on 'having put that old fox Churchill in the bag.' In his favour, besides part promises and the presence of influential British missions near his High Command – which allowed him to keep open a direct line with London – was the strategic disposition of the Allied armies in Italy. The American Fifth Army, led by General Mark Clark, was marching up the boot on the western side, while the British Eighth Army was proceeding along the eastern side. This meant that Yugoslav partisan forces would meet up with the British at the end of their advance, and not with the Americans. This detail would be of great importance when the 'race for Trieste' began.

At that time, the supreme commander of Allied forces in the Mediterranean was Marshal Alexander, an Englishman who esteemed and respected Tito. The two marshals had met several times, in Bolsena, Italy, and in Belgrade. Tito had from the first made it clear to Alexander that he absolutely insisted on the right to occupy militarily the Julian region. After lively discussions, Alexander had accepted this compromise: Tito would accept that the Allies would constitute a military government in Venezia Giulia, and they in turn would recognize the civil administrations established in the region by Slavic bodies. This compromise was not agreeable to the Americans, but they finally accepted it in the belief that the progress of the war would nullify it. They were certain, in fact, that the Allies would reach the 1939 Italian borders before the Yugoslavs.

In the spring of 1945, they found out they were wrong. Tito was quickly approaching Trieste, and the Americans were beginning to worry. They considered it indispensable to gain control of Venezia Giulia in order to guarantee their supply lines into Austria and Central Europe.

Churchill, too, began to worry about this development, and he personally asked the American president to rush toward Trieste and take the city before the Slavs could. He reminded Truman of Stalin's well-known principle, which Tito clearly followed: 'Possession is nine-tenths of the law.'

The Allies asked themselves how they should behave if Tito broke his promises and occupied Venezia Giulia, thus blocking access for the Allied armies. Churchill and Alexander disagreed strongly on this point. When the British prime minister openly considered using force to push the Yugoslavs back, Alexander responded with a harsh telegram in which he raised doubts about the 'morality' of such an order and reminded Churchill that his soldiers 'have a strong admiration for Tito's partisans and are strongly in agreement with them. One will have to think hard before asking them to forget the common enemy and fight an ally, instead.'

After an exchange of opinions between Truman and Churchill, the Allied leaders in Italy were finally instructed to proceed with haste to occupy Venezia Giulia and establish a military government over the entire region, including Fiume and the Dalmatian islands, but excluding the city of Zara.

The 'Liberation' of Zara

Zara had been the first Italian city to fall. Ninety per cent of it had been destroyed by fifty-four bombing raids that had caused thousands of deaths. This city that in language, culture, and architecture was the purest Venetian fortress on the Dalmatian coast, was a ghost town when Tito's troops entered it in November 1944. As already noted, there had been no strategic reasons to destroy it. A kerchief of land jutting out to sea, tightly built up within its Venetian architecture of *calli* and *campielli*, Zara was neither a naval base nor a military fort and was completely surrounded by Croatian territory controlled by the *Titini*. It had been besieged for months; Italian ships had only occasionally succeeded in bringing it food and medical supplies and evacuating refugees and the wounded. By September 1943 it was no longer a military objective. By then, the soldiers protecting it had largely dispersed. About one hundred Germans were left, along with a few hundred Zaratin volunteers enrolled in the armed forces of the Italian Social Republic, and a few dozen civic security guards and Carabinieri. These were already in touch with the Slavic Resistance, which had promised to treat them well when they finally took the city.

So there was no strategic need to destroy Zara and disperse its inhabitants. But the partisan leaders saw the city as a thorn in their side, as a Venetian cultural enclave on Croatian territory. So they misled the Allies by exaggerating the city's importance, thus inducing them to destroy it.

When the partisans finally entered the city, they destroyed its last Venetian vestiges. The Lions of St Mark, which for centuries had stood above its gates, were torn down. Other symbols of the ancient Venetian Republic were chiselled away. For three days, in Piazza dei Signori, Italian books were thrown into a bonfire, along with rare documents from the city's archives and files from the registry offices. The surviving Italians now faced the same bleak genocidal rituals that had already been carried out in Istria: firing squads, hangings, drownings. Dozens of civilians and Carabinieri were 'slaughtered like dogs,' according to

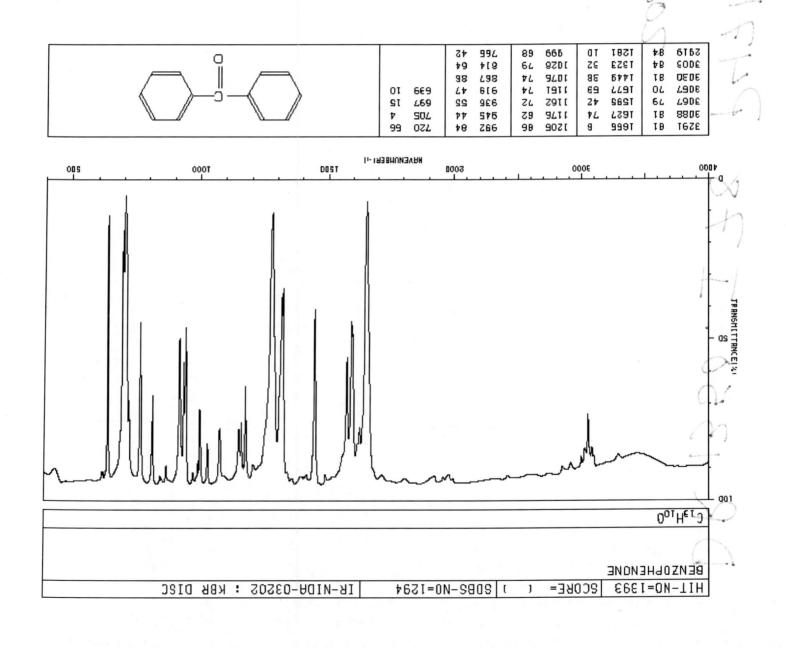

2919	84	1281	10	999	88	766	42
3003	84	1323	32	1026	79	814	64		
3030	81	1449	38	1076	74	867	86		
3067	70	1677	69	1161	74	919	47	639	10
3067	79	1595	42	1162	72	936	55	697	15
3088	81	1627	74	1176	82	945	44	705	4
3291	81	1666	6	1206	96	992	84	720	66

BENZOPHENONE

$C_{13}H_{10}O$

HIT-NO=1393 | SCORE= ( ) | SDBS-NO=1294 | IR-NIDA-O3202 : KBR DISC

the testimony of Lieutenant Antonio Calderoni, one of the few who escaped. Schoolteachers, civic employees, shopkeepers, all of them went to the wall. Pietro Luxardo (fig. 11), the distiller of the famous maraschino liqueur, disappeared forever; his brother Niccolò was thrown into the sea together with his wife Bianca, a stone around their necks.

An Italian island in Croatian Dalmatia, Zara was snuffed out. Of its 22,000 inhabitants, 4,000 died during the bombings; 2,000 others were murdered by the partisans, and the rest were forced into exile. Italian Zara no longer exists: it is a dead city. In the end, it suffered the fate wished upon it by the Croatian writer Vladimir Nazor, a great poet and a great chauvinist who, at the age of seventy, joined Tito's partisans. He had written: 'We will sweep from our land the stones of the destroyed tower of the enemy and we will throw them into the deep sea of oblivion. In place of Zara we will raise the new Zadar that will be our look-out into the Adriatic.'

'Trst je nâs!' Trieste Is Ours

Czar Nicholas has issued a decree:
Arrest the living, and let the dead go free!

Thus sang Tito's partisans as they marched into Trieste. Few words, but an entire program. It was May Day of 1945. On the various European fronts the war that had lasted nearly six years was coming to an end, but in Venezia Giulia the worst was about to begin. Twenty-four hours earlier, at 2:30 p.m., Radio London had announced that Trieste had been liberated by Yugoslav troops; immediately after that, Radio Belgrade had confirmed the news, claiming that 'all the people of Yugoslavia greet in unison this great success of our armed forces for the liberation of our Yugoslav Trieste.'

The race for Trieste had begun a few weeks earlier. The Allies now understood that in order to secure the supply lines for their troops in Austria, they would have to control the Julian territory and the ports of Trieste, Pola, and Fiume. Churchill, worried about the Red Army's rapid advances in Europe, was now pressuring General Alexander to reach Trieste before the partisans, notwithstanding any past agreements with Tito. So the Second New Zealand Division of the British Eighth Army, led by General Bernard Freyberg, made a dash for the port. But as the result of a series of confused and suspicious orders and counterorders, it would not arrive on time.

Tito had long intended to confront the Allies with a *fait accompli*. He ordered his forces to ignore all secondary objectives and concentrate on taking Trieste. At that moment, even the liberation of Yugoslav national territory was of secondary importance to Tito. In the end, his forces entered Zagreb on 8 May and Ljubljana on 11 May. Fiume and Pola, instead, were freed on 8 and 4 May respectively.

Clearly, the Yugoslavs were anxious to 'liberate' parts of the Italian territory even before they liberated their own. So that the liberation of Trieste would be a completely Yugoslav victory, the Italian Natisone, Fontanot and Trieste brigades, which had been inserted into the Slovenian IX Korpus, had been transferred inland some time before to help liberate Ljubljana. Only later, on 20 May, to assuage the anger of the disillusioned Garibaldini, would the three formations be allowed to enter Trieste.

On 1 May 1945, Tito could thus attribute the liberation of the Julian capital to his own troops, even though, truth be told, Trieste had already liberated itself. On 28 April, after the German surrender was announced in Italy, young Italians had flooded the city's streets waving Italian flags. At the same time, during a meeting of the prefecture, the Fascist prefect Bruno Coceani had transferred 'power' to the president of the Trieste National Liberation Committee, Antonio De Berti. Afterwards, Coceani had proposed the creation of a united Italian front against the Slavs, one that would unite what was left of the forces of the Social Republic with those of the National Liberation Committee. This offer was rejected. It was unthinkable that after months and months of civil war, Fascists and anti-Fascists could instantly erase all that divided them on the political front, even for the sake of the Motherland. One should also not forget that an Italo-Slovenian Communist cell was operating in Trieste (the most combative one, to boot), and that it would have denounced that promiscuity as high treason.

In the few days that preceded the entry of Tito's forces into the city, confusion reigned in Trieste. The Germans, knowing what would happen if the *Titini* captured them, locked themselves in their barracks, determined to surrender only to the Allied army; meanwhile, three different formations of insurgents were moving around the town without any coordination among them. The men of the Civic Guard, the militia, the Carabinieri, and the Guardie di Finanza all wore a tricolour armband; the Italian partisans of the National Liberation Committee wore a tricolour rosette; and the Italo-Slovenian Communists wore a beret with a red star. Relations among these three formations were not smooth: there were even armed clashes between them.

The Trieste National Liberation Committee found itself in an awkward position. In other Italian cities that had risen up, the local committee had been able to bring together all the anti-Fascist parties and coordinate their actions. The Trieste Committee, in contrast, had been abandoned by the Communists (who had then joined with the Slavs); even so, it had no choice but to consider the political strength of the Italian Communist Party. In this contradiction lay its weakness, which grew greater still when it was forced to choose: to ally itself with the Fascists in order to fight the Slavs, or join with the Italo-Slovenian Liberation Front and welcome Tito's troops as liberators.

After a stormy debate, the Trieste committee chose the second option. Its members were hoping (in vain, it turned out) that the arrival of the Allies would slow down or hinder the Slavic occupation of the city. On the evening of 30 April, it was still not clear which side would arrive first, and wild rumours were circulating. Radio London added to the confusion by announcing at 2:30 p.m. that the Yugoslavs had liberated Trieste. This announcement was followed by a statement by Palmiro Togliatti, who, clearly taking for granted the entry of Tito's troops into the city, sent Triestinians his brotherly greeting, urging them to avoid 'at all costs falling victim to provocateurs interested only in sowing discord' between Italians and Yugoslavs. That night, many Triestinians did not sleep: the following day, the fate of their city would be decided.

On the morning of 1 May, while Yugoslav troops were entering Trieste, the New Zealand division of General Freyberg reached Monfalcone, which had already been occupied by the Slovenian IX Korpus. This first encounter between the Allies and the *Titini* was not at all festive, as one can imagine. The Slavs openly indicated their displeasure at the arrival of the British forces on 'their' territory and sought in every way to obstruct it. Only after a lengthy exchange of radio messages between top officers, and many hours of negotiations (the secret results of which would be reflected in the puzzling behaviour of the British during the Yugoslav occupation of Trieste), was Freyberg authorized to proceed. His forces entered Trieste on the afternoon of 2 May. The following day, Gorizia was liberated by British troops.

The arrival of the British in Trieste rekindled the hopes of the civilian population and led the Germans, still locked inside their strongholds, to plead for the right to surrender. Within a few hours, 2,700 prisoners were rounded up.

At this point, Operation Trieste had been completed from a military perspective. However, the political clashes were about to begin. The Slavs demanded the 'return' of the 2,700 German prisoners on the grounds that they had been captured on territory previously occupied by the Yugoslavs. Freyberg, in spite of the commitment he had made at the moment of the surrender, bowed to this demand and handed the prisoners over to the Slavs, who shipped them, along with hundreds of soldiers from the Italian Social Republic, to the notorious prison camps of Abbazia, Susak, and Crikvenica. The Ustachi, Domobranci, and Chetnik formations that had been pushed into Venezia Giulia by the Yugoslav advance would encounter a worse fate even than this.

The Yugoslav command broke the promises it had made to the Trieste National Liberation Committee – the same promises that had induced the committee to join with the Italo-Slovenian Front. We will speak later about what happened in Trieste during those horrible forty days of Yugoslav occupation.

Having won the race for Trieste, Tito's forces charged past the Allies to occupy militarily what was left of Istria and Dalmatia. Everywhere atrocities were committed against Italians, and columns of desperate people took to the roads in a forced exodus.

The *Titini* entered Fiume on 3 May, over strong resistance from a few units of the Tenth left to defend the city after the retreat of the Germans. In the meantime, Fiume had passed into the control of volunteers organized by the local National Liberation Committee; these, however, were quickly brushed aside. When the Slavic troops entered the city, the frightened citizens locked themselves into their houses, dreading the intentions of the Slavs, whom they did not see as liberators.

Their fears, unfortunately, were well founded. On the night of 4 May, after the curfew imposed by the military command, the secret police (OZNA), assisted by paramilitary bands headed by a sinister figure, the Fiuman Oskar Piskulic – called 'the Yellow One' because of the colour of his skin – began eliminating the leaders of the anti-annexation faction. The bloodbath had begun. Slaughters, *foibe*, firing squads, and deportations would continue for several months, until the surviving Italians fled their homes and abandoned their belongings and sought refuge in Italy.

Pola was attacked on 4 May. The following day, the German troops received the order to lock themselves into the fortress there and resist until the arrival of the Allies, to whom they would surrender. For several days, the few Italian units of the Tenth defended their positions ferociously, until after a series of bloody clashes, starting on 6 May they began to surrender. Their fate would be horrible. Those who survived the *foibe* and the indiscriminate firing squads faced an extremely harsh captivity marked by starvation and disease.

In the days that followed, watched by the terrified civilians of Pola (who were overwhelmingly Italian), the Slavs organized displays of frenzied nationalism, to the cheers of local Communists. For days on end, the streets were filled with military parades, which were applauded on command by hordes of Croatian farmers trucked in from the countryside. A People's Liberation Committee was set up, and a Polesan worker, Francesco Neffat, was called upon to head it. From that moment on, he began to call himself Franjo Nefat.

In Pola, just as in Fiume and in the other towns of Istria and Dalmatia, the hunt for Italians began. By night, hundreds of Italians were methodically taken from their homes. The occupiers tried to work quietly, but failed. The arrests, which were carried out with the help of local informers, gave rise to suspicion and panic among Italians. Only after 12 June, after Alexander and Tito signed an agreement to transfer Trieste, Gorizia, and Pola to the Allies, could the citizenry of Pola begin to wake up from their forty-day nightmare.

Ethnic Cleansing and Political Cleansing

Italians were not the only ones to flee the unleashed fury of Tito's troops and of the paramilitary bands at their side. Slavs of various ethnic backgrounds who had collaborated with the Germans or who opposed the new regime suffered an even worse fate. The luckier ones were the Chetniks, 'legal' or not.

By the end of April 1944, it was obvious that the Nazis would soon be defeated, and long columns of armed men, with their wives and children, and with their belongings bundled on mules or carts, began moving west from the various regions of Yugoslavia. They had fought alongside the Germans and had committed every kind of horror. Now the bill was due, and they were hoping to save themselves by seeking asylum under the Allies. Pursued by Tito's troops, they cleared the road ahead of them by force of arms, leaving behind a smoking trail of sacked and destroyed villages.

Toward the end of April, a formation of Chetniks descended from Slovenia to the gates of Gorizia. This long column was 20,000 strong, many thousands of them armed. Most of them were Serbian, but there were also Montenegrins, Slovenians, and Dalmatians of various political stripes, all of them drawn together by their fear of reprisals by the *Titini*. They included collaborationist Chetniks, semi-collaborationist Chetniks (that is, those who had agreed to fight against the Communists but not against the Allies), and diehard Chetniks still loyal to King Peter II and to General Mihajlović.

Weapons in hand, gleaming knives in their belts, and long hair down to their shoulders, the Serbians fell on the first houses they saw, sacking them and attacking the defenceless citizens. Many women were raped, and panic spread throughout Gorizia. By then, the Germans and the units of the Italian Social Republic that had been holding the city had withdrawn. Fortunately, there were still 250 Carabinieri, led by Lieutenant Tonnarelli, who continued to provide public safety. The Carabinieri, assisted by volunteers from the local National Liberation Committee, bravely confronted the invading horde. The clashes continued for three days, from 29 April to 1 May, when the Serbians withdrew, leaving a trail of blood behind. The Chetnik horde now headed toward eastern Friuli, where they camped around the city of Palmanova, near the British lines. Discussions for their surrender continued for days. Tito's envoys were demanding that they be handed over to them; the Chetniks countered with the demand that they be recognized as soldiers of General Draža Mihajlović and granted the safe-conduct the Allies had once promised him. In the end, common sense prevailed: the British knew that most of these men were collaborationists, but refused to hand them over to Tito's forces. After disarming them, they transferred the Chetniks to a prisoner-of-war camp near Forlì, where they remained for a year. Later, they would be released to immigrate overseas or to other European countries. This humane treatment, so very different from what was meted out to other prisoners, was a reflection of Britain's sense of guilt for 'betraying' Mihajlović in favour of Tito.

The Croatian Ustachi and Slovenian Domobranci fared far worse. The scythe of 'political cleansing' cut them down like a field of grain. Hundreds of thousands died.

The Croatian and Slovenian collaborationists had committed acts of ferocious evil and knew that the vengeance of the *Titini* would be unforgiving. So they sought refuge *en masse* in the Austrian valleys between Bleiburg and Loibach, hoping to surrender to British troops. This time, however, the British would not be moved. According to the Yalta agreements, vanquished armies were to deal directly with their respective victors; thus, the Ustachi and Domobranci were handed over to the Yugoslav government. This decision led to heart-rending scenes in the refugee camps. Thousands committed suicide. Those who did not were forced into sealed wagons. In this way, 300,000 Ustachi were handed over to Tito's troops and shipped to Yugoslavia.

The slaughter began as soon as they crossed the border. The number of dead reached unimaginable levels. According to testimony gathered by the historian Pier Arrigo Carnier, 75,000 Croatians were killed near Maribor and buried in vast common graves. For days, people in the area heard the crackle of machine guns. Another 30,000 Ustachi were shot in the forest of Kocevlje. Thousands more Croatians, but also Serbians, Montenegrins, and Slovenians, died of exhaustion during the 'march of death' toward the labour camps near the border with Greece and Romania. Few survived the bloodbath. One of them was Poglavnik Ante Pavelić, the only collaborationist leader in Europe to survive the Second World War. Protected by important members of the Croatian clergy, he sought refuge in Rome in the monastery of San Geronimo. Later, he immigrated to Argentina. He died in Madrid in 1959 surrounded by some of his most faithful Ustachi, who had followed him into exile.

The Slovenian Domobranci met the same fate as the Ustachi. With cold determination, the English returned them to the Yugoslavs, who slaughtered them in the forests of Slovenia. It is estimated that more than 12,000 died. Several thousand collaborationist Serbians, Bosnians, and Montenegrins were killed alongside them.

A similar fate fell on the Volksdeutsche, the 'Aryans' whom the VOMI had plucked from the Yugoslavian ethnic muddle to serve as soldiers of the Reich. They were all eliminated.

Coldly determined to respect the Yalta agreements, the British handed over to the Soviets the 60,000 Cossacks of Carnia and Croatia, who had sought refuge along the high Drava River. At the moment of the handover, hundreds of Cossacks threw themselves into the river in a collective suicide. The others were slaughtered or deported.

In his memoirs, Alexander made no mention of this appalling extermination, which took place during peacetime yet spilled more blood than the entire Italian campaign.

The Forty Days of Trieste

'Trst je nâs!' shouted masses of farmers brought into the city from the countryside in a whirl of Slovenian flags and red flags (but many more Slovenian ones than red ones). Trieste is ours! Bands played, militiamen marched, and a few spectators with red neckerchiefs applauded.

From behind their windowshades, Triestinians watched with dismay these loud celebrations, which were held two or three times a day. The arrival of the New Zealanders, whom an enormous crowd had welcomed with a sea of tricolours, had not changed the situation. In the

hearts of Triestinians, apprehension soon replaced hope. On the afternoon of 2 May, General Freyberg, who had set up his command in the
Hôtel de Ville, had received the members of the National Liberation
Committee, which had set itself up in the Palace of the Prefecture as the
legitimate representative of the Italian government. That conversation
proved disappointing. Freyberg turned down the committee's request
that he assume political and military control over the city. He explained
to them that according to signed agreements, the Yugoslavs had allowed him to enter Trieste as a 'guest,' and that he would behave as a
'guest' until he received other orders. Disappointed, the leaders of the
Trieste committee left the Hôtel de Ville with the clear sense that the
Allies now viewed their city as part of the Yugoslav state.

For forty very long days Trieste would be, to all intents and purposes,
a Yugoslav city. For Triestinians, consequences would be tragic.

On 3 May, the Yugoslav military command issued its first decrees.
Although the war had ended, a state of war was nevertheless proclaimed, and many were called up (these recruits would then be sent to
Croatia for the purpose of 'lightening the Italianness of the region').
Martial law was declared, and a strict curfew was imposed from 3 p.m.
until 10 a.m. Standard time was adjusted to match the time in Belgrade
and thus harmonize Trieste with 'the rest of Yugoslavia.' The National
Liberation Committee was immediately stripped of its powers. Its decrees were annulled, and its leaders were pursued. The new mayor of
the Liberation, Michele Miani, ended up in jail, and the president of the
National Liberation Committee, Antonio De Berti, and other leaders
went into hiding. So did many Italian partisans who had refused to
hand in their weapons. Freedom of the press, which had resurfaced
only a few days earlier, was suppressed again. Only the Communist
daily, directed by Mario Pacor, was still being published, and its name
had an ominous ring for Triestinians: *Nostro Avvenire* (Our Future). This
news sheet, which was completely in tune with Slavic positions, launched
a violent defamatory campaign against the patriots of the National
Liberation Committee, who were dismissed as 'agents of the Gestapo
and Fascists.'

The Yugoslavs paid special attention to the banks. All safety deposit
boxes were sealed, and all chequing and savings accounts were frozen.
Control over them was assigned to Slovenian commissars. The Bank of
Italy was declared liquidated and replaced by the Yugoslav National
Bank. In late May and early June, 160 million lire were taken 'on the
orders of the Slovenian government.'

In the wake of these decrees, the secret police, the OZNA, were unleashed to do their work, supported by the 'People's Guards.' The tricolours put out by the population to greet the New Zealanders were torn or machine-gunned down, and all Italian symbols were effaced. All who declared themselves Italian, including those who had fought and suffered in the Resistance, were assumed to be Fascists and enemies of the people. Only those who accepted the Yugoslav party line were considered to be good, democratic citizens.

On 5 May, in response to one of the many pro-Yugoslav demonstrations organized by trucking into the city Slovenian activists from the countryside, thousands of Triestinians filled the streets waving tricolours. A procession formed spontaneously behind a group of young students, and marched peacefully along the Corso, singing the national anthem, growing all the while. Then, at via Imbriani, Tito's militia appeared and without warning opened fire on the crowd. The demonstrators scattered, leaving five dead and dozens of wounded on the street. Many New Zealand soldiers witnessed the shooting, but confined themselves to taking photographs of the event.

While all this was happening, General Freyberg, isolated in his command post at the Hôtel de Ville, surrounded by Frisian horses and armoured personnel carriers, continued to receive politely various delegations of citizens but took no action. He did not bat an eye even when, on 9 May, General Dušan Kveder, commander of the Yugoslav forces, announced from the balcony of the city hall, to the applause of the crowd below: 'Trieste was liberated by the Yugoslav army and it is our intention to unite it, Pola, and Fiume, to the Yugoslav state.' Freyberg would remain neutral throughout all these horrible forty days of the city's occupation by the *Titini*.

In his memoirs, Winston Churchill does not explain why or how the British soldiers were forced to become silent spectators of anti-Italian barbarism. He does, however, admit sorrowfully: 'In Venezia Giulia our men were forced to watch, with no possibility of intervening, deeds that offended their sense of justice and they felt this was tacit acquiescence to the misdeed.'

The People's Guards Sow Terror

And so Trieste lost its freedom even before it had regained it. Slavic repression fell on Fascists and collaborationists, but these were only a small minority of the victims. In reality, the Yugoslav plan for Trieste and for all of Venezia Giulia was to fall on everything that was Italian. As Antonio Pitamitz tells it, the first to be picked up by the People's Guards were the Guardie di Finanza, the customs and excise officers who with the Carabinieri had supported the Resistance and helped liberate the city alongside the volunteers of the National Liberation Committee. With their disappearance, the last strong presence of the Italian state disappeared from the city.

The Italians who were arrested, when they were not quickly thrown into the *foibe* after mock trials, were deported to the plateau of the Carso or to concentration camps in Slovenia that have remained embossed on the memory of those who returned alive. In the area of Basovizza, anyone who tried to escape was shot. Another form of punishment was the 'post,' from which prisoners were left dangling until they lost the use of their limbs. Prisoners were killed for a trifle: the theft of a potato, a flash of anger ... In the prison camp of Boroviza, the partisan Giovanni Nalon, from the Garibaldi Brigade, died of hardship. Before being shot and thrown into the *foibe*, the partisans Bruno Mineo, Luigi Berti, Stefano Pirnetti, Federico Buzzai, and Carlo Dell'Annunziata, and many others who had fought in the non-Communist formations of 'Justice and Liberty,' passed through the same camp. Many nameless Italian soldiers just returned from the German concentration camps and arrested without cause by Tito's partisans also met their death here.

The Guardie di Finanza who disappeared were certainly more than the ninety-seven officially listed as dispersed. The testimony of sailor Angelo D'Ambrosio sheds light on the possible fate of many others. During those days, he saw in the vicinity of San Pietro del Carso a column of 180 Guardie di Finanza pass by, escorted by *Titini* partisans. They told him they were heading for a concentration camp, but that night, D'Ambrosio heard the crackling of machine-gun fire. The following day, the sailor saw six trucks go by full of half-naked bodies, followed a little later by *Titini* partisans wearing the uniforms of the Guardie di Finanza, complete with rank insignia and decorations.

In occupied Trieste, Villa Segré, headquarters of a flying squad of People's Guards, acquired a sinister reputation. This unhappy villa was coloured red, not black. Horrendous things happened inside. The prisoners were often forced to fight each other in order to amuse their jailers. The customary punishment was to shove the unfortunate victim's head in the excrement bucket. Prisoners were tortured and killed without pity. An Italian woman was forced to clean the floors with an Italian flag. Professor Elena Pezzoli, a member of the National Liberation

Committee, was tortured at length and then thrown in a *foiba*. The horror the People's Guards inflicted on the city was such that the Yugoslav authorities were obliged to intervene. The torturers were all arrested and some were shot. They were all Italian.

In the meantime, even in Trieste the mass executions at the *foibe* had begun. Italians were dumped by the hundreds into those enormous chasms, which descend hundreds of metres into the carsic rock. Soldiers of the Wehrmacht, Ustachi, and Domobranci were dumped in with them. From one *foiba* were recovered the bodies of twelve New Zealand soldiers.

The execution methods were the same as had been deployed in Istria. The prisoners were stripped naked and tied in a row with wire. They were placed in a line at the edge of the chasm, and the first few were shot. As they fell, they dragged all the rest into the *foiba*. The chain of unfortunates fell into the darkness, bouncing from one rock outcrop to the next until they struck the ground at the bottom, where the living agonized next to the dead. Often the jailers amused themselves with those who were about to die. 'Anyone who can jump across to the other side will be spared,' they promised. Someone would try to leap the chasm, but even those who succeeded were gunned down. There had to be no witnesses. Some did manage to escape death. One of them was Graziano Udovisi. This is his story, recorded by Massimo Gramellini.

Saved by a Miracle

They made me march on the brushwood with bare feet, tied with wire to a friend who, after a few steps, fainted and so I, walking along, was dragging him behind me. Then a voice yelled at me in Slavic: 'Stop!' I lowered my eyes and I saw it: a deep fissure on the ground, like an enormous pit. I was on the edge of a *foiba*. Then I understood everything: the time to die had arrived.

It all began on 5 May 1945. The war had ended, I had put down my arms and surrendered myself to the Slavic command. I was deported to a concentration camp near Pola. Before the tragedy there was the humiliation: Tito's partisans amused themselves by making me eat pieces of paper and swallow stones. Then they fired a few shots near my ear. I jumped with fear, they laughed scornfully.

Together with other companions I ended up at Pozzo Vittoria, in the school's old gym. Some of us were forced to run headlong into the wall.

They fell to the ground bleeding at the head. The Croatians kicked them till they got up again. I was punished in a different way: a frightening blow with a stick on my left ear. From that day, I can barely hear any more.

Here we were in Fianona. Late at night. This time they locked us up in an old barracks. Twenty people in a room three metres by four. To beat us, they transferred us in a larger room where a gigantic man began to punch me. *'On your feet, damn you!'* yelled the Slavic Hercules. I saw two uniforms come in and inside one of the two there was a woman. Then I turned my eyes toward my companions: their backs seemed painted red, but they were flowing with blood. *'The tallest one forward,'* the giant yelled and grabbed me by the hair and dragged me in front of the woman. She calmly pulled out her pistol and broke my jaw with the butt. She then took a wire and tightened it around our wrists, tying us in groups of two. They made us get out. The march towards the *foiba* began.

Our fate was sealed, and I had only one way of escaping it: throw myself into the precipice before I was hit by a bullet. A voice yelled in Slavic: *'Death to Fascism, freedom for the people!'* a slogan they repeated at every step. As soon as I heard the crackling of the machine gun, I threw myself into the *foiba*.

I fell on a small jutting tree. I could see nothing, the bodies were falling on top of me. I managed to free my hands from the wire and I began to climb back up. I could not breathe any longer. Suddenly my fingers touched a stump of grass. I looked more carefully: it was hair! I grabbed it and so I managed to drag another man to the surface. The only Italian who, like me, survived the *foibe*. His name was Giovanni, 'Ninni' to his friends. He died in Australia a few years ago.

For forty days the systematic slaughter of Italians continued throughout the region, raising indignation and anguish even among Slovenian civilians. But there were also those who rejoiced in it. On 5 August 1945, after the discovery of yet another *foiba*, the Slovenian daily in Trieste, *Primorski Dnevnik*, wrote: 'On the land that suffered for twenty-five years the terror of Fascist nationalization this is not the first nor will it be the last *foiba* where the bones of the Italo-Fascist criminals will be pulverized.'

Even Monfalcone was targeted by the militia charged with the 'ethnic cleansing.' Several dozen people were arrested and disappeared. The same happened in Gorizia, which had already lived through a short yet tragic Slavic occupation after 8 September and had barely escaped a second one at the hands of the Serbian Chetniks. Tito's forces entered

Gorizia on 2 May 1945 without encountering resistance, and proceeded to follow the same blueprint used in Trieste: the local National Liberation Committee was abolished, all its decrees were annulled, and the clocks were adjusted to Belgrade time. Yugoslav authorities even issued new identity cards. Anyone without one was arrested. The Italian flag was banned, and anyone who dared to display a tricolour rosette was beaten. The city was plastered with large portraits of Tito and Stalin, and on all the walls there appeared the password of the Yugoslav Resistance: *Smrt fašismu, sloboda narodu* (death to Fascism, freedom to the people).

But there was not even the shadow of freedom. The Italian press was suppressed, and all parties were banned except the Italian Communist Party, which had accepted the line that Venezia Giulia belonged to Yugoslavia. More than two hundred Carabinieri and public security guards were captured and deported. Only six would return, among them the heroic Lieutenant Tonnarelli, who had saved the city from the Chetnik marauders. Many leading figures of the Italian majority also disappeared, including many leaders of the National Liberation Committee. As Antonio Pitamitz observes, these people had rejected the 'unilateral annexation' of those lands to Yugoslavia, but they were helpless in the face of Slavic arrogance. Like the inhabitants of the Julian region, they, too, ended up paying for the illusions of the National Liberation Committee for Northern Italy, which had believed in the Yugoslavian anti-Fascist internationalism for which the Italian Communist Party had made itself the guarantor. Recognizing that action was impossible, the surviving leaders of the Gorizia National Liberation Committee disbanded their unit and left for Udine.

In Gorizia, abandoned to the occupying forces, the terror began quickly. As in Trieste, the People's Guards ran amok. They swept up hundreds of people, whose fate will never be known. On 18 May, they even entered the hospital and took away about fifty bedridden patients, saying they had to be transferred to Trieste. Nothing more would ever be known about them – not even their names, for the *Titini* burned all the hospital's files. The burning of documents – above all, municipal archives and registries – was such common practice that it must have had a specific purpose. Probably, it was to erase the records of the Italian presence, with an eye to an eventual plebiscite.

The Yugoslav powers made their mark on the life of the city. Religious services and funerals were obstructed. In cemeteries, it was decreed that a red star be erected instead of a cross, and priests who did not submit to this were persecuted. The Archbishop of Gorizia, Monsignor Carlo Margotti, who condemned the atrocities regardless of which side perpetrated them, was expelled from the city on the grounds that he was opposed to 'the movement of national liberation.'

Until now, most of the victims of the *foibe* had been townspeople or rural people. This now changed; the newest victims were mainly city dwellers. The Slavs were systematically eliminating those Italian political representatives who had fought against Fascism, but who now represented an obstacle to Belgrade's expansionist plans.

Over the forty days of the 'first' Slavic occupation, the wave of violence also fell on Pola.

In the report of the Italian government prepared for presentation at the Paris Peace Conference, one reads horrifying depositions: three hundred Italians, most of them partisans, killed with hatchets at a naval base; executioners who divide among themselves the victims' valuable possessions; bank accounts emptied; tortures and more tortures. Ambrosio Mannoni gives this testimony: 'In the jail in Buccari the men are forced to stand still at attention barefoot on pointed sticks. Pieces of iron are stuck between their fingers. They remain in this position for up to three days, howling, without food, while their feet swell. When they collapse exhausted on the ground they are forced to stand up again by beating them with rifle butts.'

'Tito, Tito, You've Ripped Us Off Quite Neat-oh'

In those days in Trieste, it was not easy to be a Communist with Italian sympathies. During the Resistance, things had been different. The common struggle, the incessant propaganda based on 'the brotherly and cordial Italo-Slovenian collaboration and on mutual respect,' the password 'death to Fascism, freedom for the people,' not to mention the suggestive parallel 'Italy = Fascism, Yugoslavia = Communism' – all of these appealed hugely to the collective imagination of the Triestinian proletariat. The Communists of Trieste had not hesitated to obey party orders and accept a subordinate position in the Yugoslav Resistance. Ideological obedience, an internationalist vision, and blind faith in Stalin and the Soviet Union had led most to underestimate the potency of Slavic nationalism and to consider it a bourgeois error or prejudice that would be overcome in time.

Doubts began to emerge among the intellectuals and the working-class élites right after the Yugoslav military occupation. Ennio Maserati, who has closely analysed the events in Trieste, notes that troubles began to surface among those who had participated in the resistance. Maserati cites the testimony of an anonymous Communist journalist in Trieste:

> A strong unhappiness began to manifest itself among the working class masses, who for ideological and political reasons were for the most part favourable to an annexation with Yugoslavia, on account of the excessive number of red-white-blue flags that kept characterizing the first demonstrations and parades in the city. They had not taken umbrage the first few days, viewing it as a legitimate outlet for the Slovenians who, after so many years of oppression and violence on the part of the Fascists, were celebrating the liberation carried out by their army. But then it had to stop, for this was becoming an expression of nationalism and the Triestinian working class had always been adverse to both nationalisms. For this reason, they expressed in growing measure this objection of theirs, putting such pressure that they forced the Slavic leaders to allow also the Italian tricolour (with a red star in it) and the red flags of the proletariat. On their part, this was a concession, since they had always fought in their ranks against the exhibition of the red and against the language of class as an expression of sectarianism, given that the partisan movement had to appear formally only as a national, democratic, and progressive movement, but not yet Communist ... The Triestinian workers took advantage of that concession and in subsequent demonstrations they descended on the streets with a large number of red flags and some Italian tricolour.

The Triestinian Communist workers, encouraged by the local federation and, albeit less adamantly, by the national leadership of the party, continued to adhere faithfully to the Yugoslav line. As late as 24 September 1945, after the Yugoslav forces left Trieste and the Free Territory was created, the local Communist federation was still repeating that the Julian Communist Party would work 'with all its strength to ensure that this territory would be assigned to the democratic and federal Republic of Yugoslavia.'

A tragic example of solidarity with the Slavic 'brothers' would be provided by workers from Monfalcone. After the exodus of Italians from Pola and Fiume, the local shipyards had been left without qualified workers. In a gesture of comradeship encouraged by the party, these workers organized a sort of counterexodus, with the intention of helping out their Yugoslav comrades by filling the vacancies left by the 'Fascists.' A dark drama, left unspoken for over half a century, then unfolded. It can be condensed into this bitter chant, voiced by the unfortunate volunteers: *Tito, Tito, te ne ga fregà pulito* (Tito, Tito, you've ripped us off quite neat-oh). We will deal later on with this tragic counterexodus.

The 'Morgan Line'

The Yugoslav military occupation of Trieste, Gorizia, and Pola ended on 12 June 1945. In the preceding terrible forty days, the Italian government, spurred on by the bishop of Trieste, Monsignor Antonio Santin, an eyewitness to and victim of Slavic high-handedness, made several attempts to induce the Allies to intervene and put an end to the bloody reprisals that were continuing even though the war had ended some time before. The Allies already knew about the ethnic and political cleansing that was underway in the Julian region controlled by Tito's forces; however, when they finally confronted Belgrade, it would be for strategic reasons, not humanitarian ones.

In the meantime, with regard to the Julian question, the positions of the British and of the Americans had nearly reversed themselves. While President Truman delayed taking action in order to maintain good relations with Stalin, Churchill, alarmed by Soviet expansion in Europe, forgot his old promises to the Yugoslavs; he now considered Tito the spearhead of Soviet penetration in the West. Because of this, he was now proposing 'a short and decisive military action' to resolve the problem by pushing the Yugoslavs back from Venezia Giulia. This plan, which risked a direct clash with the Soviet Union, met no favour among the Americans, who strongly rejected – and not just for moral reasons – the idea of complicating their already difficult relations with the Russians. At the time, the United States was still at war with Japan. Underestimating the importance of the atomic bomb, which had been built in the laboratories of Los Alamos but which had not yet been tested, Washington believed that Soviet intervention in the Pacific theatre was going to be vital to defeating Japan. At the same time, however, the Allies desperately required access to Venezia Giulia's ports and railways in order to supply their forces in central Europe.

Tito had conveniently forgotten his previous agreements with Alexander and had no intention of ceding that territory, 'whose possession was nine-tenths of the law.' Trusting in the protection of his comrade Stalin, Tito refused with a scowl all Allied overtures on this question. In the end, however, he backed down. His about-turn is unexplainable except as the result of an agreement reached behind his back between Truman and Stalin. In a speech he made in Ljubljana, Tito himself hinted at this interference in Yugoslav matters: 'We ask that each one be lord in his own house, we do not want to pay the debts of others, we do not want to be the payment coin or the exchange note for anyone.'

But Tito did pay the 'debt,' unhappily accepting Stalin's suggestion that he reach an agreement with the Allies on a demarcation line. On 9 August, an Allied delegation headed by General Morgan, Chief of Staff to General Alexander, flew into Belgrade. After heated negotiations, a line was finally drawn (later to be known as the 'Morgan Line') that divided Venezia Giulia into two occupation zones. Zone A would be administered by the Allies, Zone B by the Yugoslavs. The line started at the Austrian border east of Tarvisio, then followed a long stretch of the Isonzo River before jogging east some more to skirt Gorizia, Monfalcone, and Trieste, finally reaching the Adriatic just south of Muggia.

Geographically, Zone A was, roughly, one-sixth of the old Italian region of Venezia Giulia. The other five-sixths went to Yugoslavia. Demographically, however, it was an even split: about 450,000 inhabitants to each zone. It was also agreed that Zone A would include the enclave of Pola with a very small hinterland, as well as the harbours of Pirano, Parenzo, and Rovigno. The Allies, however, took possession only of the city of Pola; the Yugoslavs took advantage of this to grab the other three coastal towns.

The agreement declared that the Morgan Line was only 'temporary' and purely military, and would not prejudice in the least any final decision on the allocation of the two zones.

In reality, even though it was part of the Free Territory of Trieste, from 1947 on, Zone B was subjected to an intensifying process of Slavification. The Yugoslav civil administration adopted all of the same measures as the Belgrade government had imposed on other regions of the country: farms were collectivized, and industries were turned into cooperatives. Important industries, such as Arrigoni and Ampelea, which were the basis of the region's prosperity, were forced to close down and fire their employees. To integrate the economy of Zone B with that of Yugoslavia, the lira was replaced by the 'jugolira' and later with the dinar. To denationalize territory even further, two particular categories of people that were traditionally a point of reference for Italians were persecuted and driven out: teachers, and Catholic clergy. Teachers who were not party members were arrested or expelled, the charge being that they were agents of the national liberation committees; priests who had remained tied to the episcopal curia in Trieste were threatened and invited, more or less explicitly, to go away.

A sensational trial was held during which all of the Benedictine monks in Daila were accused of trading contraband and exporting money. All of the brothers were found guilty and sentenced to six months to four years of hard labour. To break all links between Zone A and Zone B, the Yugoslav civil authorities obstructed whenever possible the movements of workers who lived in Zone B but whose jobs were in Zone A. It was claimed that these people were 'spies for the National Liberation Committee.' This justified forcing them to undergo slow and meticulous searches on their daily commute.

Thus began the long agony of Zone B, which according to the peace treaty should have been divided equally according to agreements stipulated directly by Rome and Belgrade. Fully Italian cities such as Pirano, Parenzo, and Rovigno were gradually ceded to Yugoslavia, in violation of every right of the ethnic Italian population of the region. Such an unlawful appropriation would eventually enjoy juridical 'blessing' as a result of the Italo-Yugoslav accord signed in Osimo in 1975.

The Yugoslavs 'Pack Their Bags'

In any event, 12 June was a day of celebration in Trieste, Pola, and Gorizia. Neither Italy nor true freedom had returned, but at least people could sleep peacefully, without trembling in fear at a knock on the door.

While the tricolour returned to the windows and the streets filled with flag-waving processions, the Yugoslavs were getting ready to pack their bags. And they did it in the true sense of the word, taking with them all they could carry: from the patrimony of the Bank of Italy to the machinery in the factories, from hospital equipment to typewriters and office supplies.

On 13 June, an Allied military government was established in Trieste. It immediately disbanded the People's Tribunals and the People's Guards, replacing them with the Venezia Giulia Police, which was staffed by local recruits and had Italian instructors. However, its regulations and procedures were drawn from British and American police forces. All of the systems and decrees imposed by the occupying Yugoslavs were withdrawn or annulled, and Italian law in effect in the peninsula was re-established. Even Italian judicial law was brought back, except for the possibility of appeal to the Supreme Court in Rome.

Thanks to the arrival of the Allied military government, the National

Liberation Committee of Trieste could come out of hiding. Its leaders were invited to prepare plans for a municipal and a provincial administration. The aim of Colonel Francis Armstrong, the representative of the Allied Military government, was to take advantage of all political forces available for the civil administration of Zone A; however, the hostility and intransigence of the Communists and of the Slovenian front led him to seek the collaboration only of the democratic parties. Because Trieste, Pola, and Gorizia were almost solidly Italian, the setting up of democratic administration did not meet with any particular difficulties in these cities. Matters were more complicated in the smaller towns with mixed populations, so much so that the Allied authorities often had to resort to commissars.

In spite of the undeniable improvements, the situation in Trieste remained highly precarious. The atmosphere was tense, and the presence of the *Titini* could be felt in all sorts of threats and intimidations. For example, the People's Guards, although disbanded and disarmed, continued to operate clandestinely and to carry out kidnappings and illegal arrests. Thanks to the freedom of the press established by the Allied military government, the Slavs continued their chauvinistic campaign through the *Corriere di Trieste* (the old *Nostro Avvenire*) and the daily paper of the Julian Communist Party, *Il Lavoratore*. The Trieste National Liberation Committee had no publication of its own because the workers in the printing shops – because they were intimidated by the Yugoslavs or because they were Communists – refused to print 'reactionary' papers.

If in Zone A the situation was serious, in Zone B it was dire. By 12 June, more than 20,000 Italians had abandoned Istria to seek refuge in Trieste or in other Italian cities. They had fled because by now they well knew that neither the Allies nor the Italian government were going to defend them. In the enclave of Pola, the situation improved quite perceptibly on 16 June, with the arrival of the Allied troops. But as Tito's troops left, they took with them seven hundred prisoner-hostages, not to mention all of the machinery in the shipyards and in the various factories.

Yet the people of Pola did not have much to celebrate. Isolated on a patch of land surrounded by a Slavic tide, ignored or nearly so by a Motherland that already considered them lost, unable to communicate even by mail, they would live for a long time under a tense psychological seige.

In the rest of Istria, the economic situation was disastrous. The coal and bauxite mines were at a standstill as a result of the failures of the management committees that had replaced the old directors, who had been arrested; the fishing industry was reduced because of the thousands of mines infesting the waters; harvests were failing as a result of collectivization; the standard of living was plummeting. In the meantime, inflation was soaring because the new bank officials did not know the most basic economic laws, and police repression was rampant. Around this time, the journalist Silvia Sprigge wrote in the *Manchester Guardian*: 'Between Pola and Trieste the road is interrupted and inland one sees the most miserable of spectacles: groups of civilians escorted by Yugoslav soldiers advance with a tired gait towards who knows what destination. One also sees single individuals, their hands tied behind their back with steel wire, led away by armed men.'

Elections were held in Zone B on 25 November 1945 to choose the Popular Assembly and the Citizen's Committees. Just before that, an extremely harsh campaign had been orchestrated in the press to persuade Istrians to vote for the only list presented in the various towns. On the walls were painted slogans such as 'Those who do not vote are Fascists,' 'Think of your family,' and 'Those who do not vote are against us.' In Rovigno, known as 'Little Moscow,' Antonio Budicin, a Communist and the brother of the martyr Pino, whose name had been given to a partisan brigade, tried to present an independent list. The list was voided, and he was thrown in jail.

In spite of intrigues and intimidations, the election amounted to a success for the Italians. The number of abstentions was very high and so was the number of ballots that had to be voided because voters had scrawled on them insulting words against Tito and Yugoslavia. In Albona, for example, out of 1,035 voters, only 770 cast ballots, and of these, 465 were annulled.

The Peace Conference

Preliminary work for preparing the Paris Peace Conference began in London in January 1946, at a time when relations between the Allies and the Soviet Union were especially tense. With respect to the Julian question, Moscow had again drawn close to Tito, and the Soviet foreign minister, Molotov, now repeated categorically that Trieste, although inhabited mainly by Italians, must nonetheless be joined with its 'natural Yugoslavian hinterland.' Also weighing heavily was what had been decided at Yalta, where Roosevelt and Churchill had agreed with Stalin on Soviet influence over Yugoslavia and the territories the latter now claimed.

Aware that the Russians supported him, Tito felt stronger than ever and did not hesitate to flex his muscles. Between January and February, the Yugoslav divisions stationed in Zone B were increased from nine to fourteen, suggesting the possibility of a *coup de main* should the Allied commission reach a decision in favour of Italy.

Between all the denials and threats, proposals for a solution to the Trieste 'question' were flying thick and fast. Even France now entered the game, having succeeded, for no good reason, in having itself welcomed into the salon of the 'greats' of the world – the victors in the Second World War. Now, in order to be recognized as a great power, France was positioning itself as a mediator between East and West. To the three proposals for a partitioning of Venezia Giulia advanced by London, Moscow, and Washington, Paris now added a fourth.

The boundaries reflected in these proposals were all based on political rather than geographic criteria. And perhaps we do not have to add that depending on the proponent, these lines could all be interpreted differently by the two countries directly affected. So let us examine these lines, keeping in mind not so much the territory as much as the distribution of the ethnic groups:

- According to the line proposed by the Americans, Italy would be assigned 370,000 Italians and 180,000 Slavs, while 50,000 Italians would remain in Yugoslavia.
- According to the British line, 356,000 Italians and 152,000 Slavs would remain in Italy, while 64,000 Italians would remain in Yugoslavia.
- According to the French line, 294,000 Italians and 113,000 Slavs would remain in Italy, while 125,000 Italians would remain in Yugoslavia.
- According to the Soviet line, no Slavs would be left in Italy, but 600,000 Italians would be left in Yugoslavia.

As can be seen from the figures, the demarcation line most favourable to Italy was the American one; the least favourable was the Soviet one. But this was only to be expected.

What is left to be done, perhaps, is to find an answer to the most obvious question: Why was no plebiscite held?

The first to advance this obvious solution was the U.S. Secretary of State James Byrnes. His proposal immediately met with the approval of the Soviets, but not of the Italian delegation. The Italian representatives at the meetings, led by Prime Minister Alcide De Gasperi, were unable to agree among themselves. The representatives of the Julian Committee declared themselves in favour of a plebiscite, as did the bishops of Pola and Parenzo, who, although aware of the existence of a Slavic majority, were certain that a great many non-Communist Slavs, in reaction to the terror instituted by Tito's regime, would vote for Italy. De Gasperi disagreed and, for a variety of reasons, the other members of the Italian delegation stood with him. They feared that the Italian Communists might support the Slavs, who would thus win a majority even in the heavily Italian cities of Pola and Trieste; they also thought that for unfathomable reasons of national and racial character – not to mention the great pressure exercised on the population by Tito's forces – a plebiscite could favour Yugoslavia. When Giuseppe Saragat, in the name of the Italian government, definitively rejected this plan, declaring that 'to insist on a plebiscite means to work against the interest of the nation,' the people of the Julian region were bitterly shocked.

The disturbing decision to reject the referendum, which most probably would have favoured Italy, and which in any case would have respected the principle of the self-determination of people, so strongly supported at that time, was later criticized from various angles. The best interpretation seems to be the one advanced by Paola Romano, who, in her careful analysis of the Julian question (see the bibliography), points out that at that time, the major preoccupation of the deputy from Trento, the Honourable Alcide De Gasperi, was the danger that a plebiscite in Venezia Giulia might lead to a plebiscite in Trentino–Alto Adige, a predominantly German-speaking region where the results would certainly have been unfavourable to Italy and favourable to Austria.

Probably, the plebiscite was rejected for other reasons besides this one. However, as the Istrian writer Pier Antonio Quarantotti Gambini notes, the fact remains that in those years the people of Venezia Giulia felt they were being used as tokens in a power game, not only by the Allies but also by Rome. Furthermore, it must be noted that the Italian representatives at the Peace Conference spent more effort on saving the fleet and on retaining the pre-Fascist colonies of Libya, Eritrea, and Somalia than on protecting Italy's eastern borders.

A More 'Rational' Ethnic Cleansing

Throughout all of 1946 and most of 1947, in the parts of Istria occupied by the Slavs, ethnic cleansing not only intensified but also became more 'rational,' in this sense: the slaughters were now aimed clearly at Italians from all social classes and from all political affiliations. The bloody events in the wake of 8 September 1943 could perhaps be described as the outcomes of popular rage or political reprisal (Togliatti, for example, would not hesitate to define them as 'a summary justice carried out by Italians themselves against Fascists'); now, there were no such excuses. The aim of the new approach was obvious even to less careful observers. The intention was to eliminate or drive from Istria as many Italians as possible and to alter the region's ethnic fabric, in case the peace conference called for a census or a plebiscite.

That said, events in Bosnia and in Kosovo in the 1990s confirm that ethnic cleansing is a tragically regular event in the racial struggles that periodically bathe the Balkans in blood. What we saw in the 1990s in Bosnia and Kosovo was merely a repetition of what had already been done fifty years earlier in Istria, the only difference being that the land did not offer the 'advantage' of *foibe* in which to hide the bodies; thus, the murderers had to rely on mass graves, easily identifiable by aerial reconnaissance.

The fable that the *foibe* were 'tombs for Fascists' – a fable that even many Italian historians have long accepted – has been disproved by authoritative Yugoslav sources. One of these is Milovan Gilan, a Serbian intellectual, who during the partisan war was the right hand of Tito, and who afterwards became a bitter adversary of the marshal. In an interview released to the magazine *Panorama* in 1991, Gilas recounts that in 1946 he personally went to Istria with Edward Kardelj, then Yugoslav foreign minister, to organize the anti-Italian propaganda so as to emphasize that that territory belonged to Yugoslavia. He explained to the magazine: 'Our purpose was to use all kinds of pressures to induce all Italians to leave. And so we did.'

We know what they did. In March 1946, when a quadripartite commission (Americans, British, French, and Russians) visited Zone B, Tito's authorities resorted to force to prevent Italians from showing themselves; at the same time, they filled the centres visited by the commission with hoards of Slovenian and Croatian farmers bussed and trucked in from the countryside. Calls by the Italian government and by the National Liberation Committee to guarantee Italians freedom of expression came to nothing. In Pirano, women crowded around the commission's cars and surreptitiously opened the palms of their hands to show the delegates the Italian flags they had painted on them. In Pisino, during a meeting, the delegates found on their tables this mysterious note: 'Unable to ask the living, go ask the dead.' Someone grasped the sense of this dark message, and the commission asked to visit the cemetery. There, they found that 90 per cent of the tombstones had Italian names carved on them. Not surprisingly, in the days that followed, all Istrian cemeteries were vandalized, and the tombstones were either removed or replaced with new ones written in Croatian.

In order to slavicize the region thoroughly, hordes of Italian farmers were forcibly transported to the Banat, their places taken by Bosnian and Macedonian farmers 'not polluted by long proximity with Italians.' Catholic priests suffered many torments and persecutions. The bishop of Trieste and Capodistria, Monsignor Antonio Santin, was assaulted several times when, ignoring the threats, he visited the parishes of his diocese situated in Zone B. The Bishop of Pola and Parenzo, Monsignor Raffaele Radossi, was arrested, stripped naked, searched, and interrogated for several days before he was released. Other priests, not only Italian ones but also Slovenian and Dalmatian, were deported and were not heard from again.

The point of all this was to terrorize Italians into leaving Istria. For some time, columns of desperate people, quite similar to the ones in Bosnia and Kosovo seen more recently on television, had been arriving at the borders of Zone A, seeking asylum in Trieste and in other Italian cities. By the eve of the signing of the peace treaty, the exodus of Italians had become a torrent. Already more than thirty thousand refugees had found asylum in refugee centres, which were not, one must say, very welcoming.

Yet these unfortunate people, who were paying the costs of the Fascists' war on behalf of all Italians, were not welcomed in Italy. Leftists, for example, viewed the refugees with suspicion and treated them like unwanted guests. Their escape from 'democratic' Yugoslavia seemed a clear denunciation of the Communist regime that was installed there. Their dramatic stories were declared base lies. The Italians in Venezia Giulia had been generically classified by the Slavs as 'Fascists'; now, so too were the Istrian refugees in Italy. One disturbing detail: the government of the Social Republic in Salò had assigned to the Julian refugees a living allowance, which was subsequently abolished and replaced by another, which lasted for only three months.

Notwithstanding the dark terror of those times in Istria, most Italians still hesitated to separate themselves from their homes and their lands. Hope is the last to die, and many Italian Istrians based their hopes in the peace conference where, perhaps with the establishment of the Free Territory of Trieste, the Julian population might find some help. But as the months went by, their dejection increased. Attempts by the Italian government to save Istria were weak and unconvincing, and the feeling grew that the game was irremediably lost. Little by little, all illusions disappeared. The Yugoslavs were ready to jump and had detailed plans at the ready. On the eve of the signing of the Peace Treaty, Italians in the region were living, as described in a note sent to the Italian foreign ministry, 'in a state of spiritual depression, apathy, uncertainty, and desperation, because Venezia Giulia is the only region that is paying for the peace and is effectively suffering the consequences of the war.'

In Paris, Vyšinskij Insults Italy

Referring to the Paris Peace Conference, where the future of Venezia Giulia was on the table, the Italian ambassador Pietro Quaroni noted: 'Perhaps it's a professional deformation, but I am unable to believe in the goodwill of America, England, and Russia towards Italy. So, when America, England and Russia rise up to defend us in anything, my response – and it's a grave sin, I know – is not a feeling of gratefulness, but the need to find out what special interests of its own that particular country is protecting or advancing when it purports to be protecting ours.' Pietro Quaroni forgets to include France. It had no territorial interests of its own in the question and was acting only for appearances' sake, yet in the end France was able, with a political agenda that Italian diplomacy characterized as 'not hostile, but unfavourable,' to see its proposal for a demarcation line triumph. After the Soviet proposal, the French one was certainly the least favourable to Italy.

Quaroni's scepticism was more than justified. Setting aside diplomatic fictions and promises of protection made to one side or the other, the decisions of the four great powers did not at all consider the demands or the aspirations of the two countries involved. Italy and Yugoslavia were pawns in a chess game that stronger powers were playing for much higher stakes than the fate of the Julian population. Moscow still considered Yugoslavia a satellite state in the developing Soviet empire; behind this attitude lay the centuries-old Russian dream of an outlet to the Mediterranean. Meanwhile, the United States and Great Britain were looking to make Trieste the 'Gibraltar of the Adriatic' and to establish it as a defensive bulwark at the only square on the entire Mediterranean chessboard from which the Red Army might move in the not unlikely case of a Third World War.

In this context, which the intensification of the Cold War rendered ever more topical, long and complicated negotiations were conducted over many months. On the excuse of defending the interests of Yugoslavia or Italy, the Anglo-Americans and the Russians carried on their game, using Venezia Giulia as a pawn. Over the course of the Paris conference, the Italian and Yugoslav representatives were invited to speak. Edward Kardelj emphatically repeated the accusations against Italy, emphasizing the war crimes carried out by Italian troops during the Fascist invasion. He repeated that Venezia Giulia was geographically part of the Balkan Peninsula and that the large Italian towns and cities of the region were nothing more than 'foreign islands in a Croatian and Slovenian sea.' Finally, he set out once again the Slavic demands already advanced in 1944, maintaining that the only border acceptable to Belgrade was, with small modifications, the one traced by the Italo-Austrian border before the First World War. He concluded by claiming that it would be a Fascist move to give a vanquished country such as Italy any territorial concessions at the expense of a victorious country such as Yugoslavia.

The presentation by Alcide De Gasperi was much more sedate. His position as the representative of a vanquished country did not, in any case, allow him to take any other approach. And so he began his speech with this somewhat pathetic statement: 'In taking the floor in this world assembly, I feel that everything, except your personal courtesy, is against me.' Then, after recalling the contribution to the defeat of Nazism and Fascism made by the Italian Resistance, he pointed out that many Italian soldiers deported to Yugoslavia were still interned in camps, even though the Alexander–Tito agreement had stipulated their immediate repatriation. He pointed out that many Italian soldiers had fought alongside the Yugoslav partisans, 'washing ancient offences away with this pledge of blood,' and he recognized that in the end, because of the mixing of the population, there was no clear ethnic line in the region. He then asked for urgent measures for Istria to correct the negative economic repercussions of the 'Morgan Line.' This line, De Gasperi underlined, has separated about 200,000 Italians from their Motherland. They would certainly be expelled or induced to abandon their own homes.

In this speech, Alcide De Gasperi officially declared that he was taking as a basis for future discussions the 'Wilson Line' proposed by the American president at the end of the First World War.

The other Italian representative, Ivanoe Bonomi, having recognized the responsibility of Fascism, and having sketched a historical time line that highlighted the Italianness of the Julian region, recommended as a last request that at least Pola, the Brioni islands, and those of Lussino be retained as part of the Free Territory of Trieste.

The Russian representatives were as harsh as the Yugoslav ones, and did not fail to call for a 'punitive peace' for Italy, which had been guilty of invading with its German ally not only Yugoslavia but Russia as well. The Soviet delegation was led by Andreij Vyšinskij, the notorious mastermind of the Stalinist purges, which had sent nearly all the leaders of the Bolshevik Communist Party to death. Vyšinskij delivered an extremely violent concluding statement against Italy, one that he laced with insults and personal attacks. He recast the history of the First World War in order to claim that Italy had not contributed to the fall of the central European empires; rather, it had engaged in 'a disloyal politic, hypocritical, false, mercenary, and definable as a politic of jackals,' and it had done the same again in the Second World War. He called the Treaty of Rapallo, whereby in 1920 Italy and Yugoslavia had freely established the new borders between them, as a 'theft against Yugoslavia.' He suggested that Italian generals were 'like ancient Roman heros as much as an ass can be like a lion' and that the Italian army was 'better at foot races than at battles.' He did not spare Alcide De Gasperi from his heavy sarcasm, but he saved his strongest fire for old Ivanoe Bonomi, whom he called 'a traitor of the people,' remembering – as if it were a grievous crime – that in 1911, Bonomi had been expelled from the Italian Socialist Party because he had supported the Libyan campaign. Vyšinskij brought his vehement concluding statements to an end by repeating that Trieste and Istria belonged, without question, to Yugoslavia.

The Cynical 'Exchange' Proposed by Togliatti

A few weeks later, to make amends for the general popular indignation at Vyšinskij's harsh words, which had caused anguish even in Leftist circles, Palmiro Togliatti travelled to Belgrade to meet Tito. On 6 November 1946, on his return to Italy, Togliatti gave a sensational interview to the Communist daily *L'Unità*. The article was titled 'Long Live the Italian–Yugoslav Understanding.' In it the Secretary of the Italian Communist Party announced that Marshal Tito was willing to leave Trieste to Italy if, in exchange, Italy would leave Gorizia to Yugoslavia.

The 'cynical exchange,' as Togliatti's proposal was quickly branded in the Italian press, raised doubts even among the Left and especially within the Italian Socialist Party, which at that time was linked to the Italian Communist Party by a binding 'agreement.' Pietro Nenni, the Socialist leader, wrote in his diary at that time: 'A day full of events. The fault is Togliatti's who, returning from Belgrade last night, rushed to give *L'Unità* a sensational interview in which he announced that Tito is prepared to give up what he does not have and asks for what we have.' And then: 'Is this all genuine? In the meantime, I will try to figure out what good for the country can be drawn from this Togliatti bombshell. The harsh, naked truth is that Tito has Stalin behind him who does not want the Americans in the Adriatic.'

Togliatti's proposal had no support. The Allies ignored it and carried on with their discussions until 20 January 1947, when the Paris Peace Conference finally determined the borders of Italy and of the Free Territory of Trieste on the basis of the line proposed by the French.

The new border left Italy with Monfalcone and Gorizia, which Italian troops would be entitled to enter the moment the treaty was signed. However, on 16 September 1947, when the Italians did move in, the Yugoslavs refused to abandon several strategic posts on the western slope of Mt Kolovrat. Several border skirmishes ensued, during which the Italian army several times gave 'an obvious display of inefficiency.' One episode among many. In the village of Crobolo, which according to the French line belonged to Italy, a Bosnian sergeant with a handful of men refused to cede the ground to the Italians. To convince him to cede it, force would have been necessary, but the Italian commander, uncertain of what to do, asked his superiors for instructions. His request followed the chain of command until it reached the desk of the Italian Minister of Foreign Affairs, Carlo Sforza, who got himself out of the tricky situation with this ineffable answer: 'You don't really want to start a Third World War just because of this hard-headed Bosnian sergeant, do you?' And this is how Gad, like many other border towns, became Yugoslav 'pockets' in Italian territory and have remained so to the present day.

After eighteen months of exhausting negotiations, an agreement was reached on 10 February 1947. The delegates of the Italian government agreed to sign the Paris Peace Treaty, which deprived Italy of Istria, including the enclave of Pola. Over the following days, the Allied troops that protected this city were withdrawn, yielding their positions to the new occupiers. For the citizens of Pola, the exodus was about to start.

3

Goodbye Istria

The Exodus from Pola

'Pola, February 1947. These days, whoever arrives in Pola finds a per-
plexing spectacle in front of him,' wrote Tommaso Besozzi in a master-
ful article from Istria for the Italian weekly *L'Europeo*:

Everywhere the signs of departure, and there is no doubt that this is a
nearly total departure. Thirty thousand out of thirty-four thousand have
asked to be transferred to Italy and thirty thousand will, in fact, abandon
their houses before Pola is handed over to Tito's soldiers. Along the docks,
from Scoglio Ulivi to nearly as far as the Arsenal, there are enormous piles
of furniture. The snow has covered them. At the train station other piles of
household furniture and fittings await. Walking along the streets of Pola,
one hears hammering coming from every house. In Venice there is a
separate office of the Italian Cabinet charged with the logistical organization of the exodus. A week ago, a telegram stamped 'Absolute precedence'
was delivered to this office. It said: 'Pola without nails and rods. Demand
you look after this with utmost urgency.' So, leaving for its first voyage,
the ship *Toscana* carried in its stowage four tons of nails and many cubic
metres of packing stakes. It arrived at the mouth of the port in Pola; a
motorboat drew up and from the ship they threw down the Jacob's-ladder
for the pilot; but the pilot kept holding the side of the ladder and they
heard him yell up: 'The nails?' The captain did not know what the pilot
was talking about. He remained speechless. 'The nails, the nails?' the irate
pilot kept on asking. Finally, the boatswain, who was directing the ma-
noeuvre, came out from a cloud of steam and reported that in the stowage
there were one hundred and sixty bags heavier than lead: given that they

did not contain meringues, one could well believe they contained nails. Only then did the pilot climb on board and inform the captain that, if he liked, he could give the order to his machinist to proceed 'slow ahead' ...

Day after day the houses in Pola empty out. Nineteen Italians out of twenty are leaving. Day after day from the countryside the Slavs move in: those who have been living for many years in the suburbs and those that constantly sneak through the 'line.' They go occupy the best dwellings in the centre of town and by the port ... The daily *L'Arena di Pola* is still being printed, but for some time now one reads only news about the exodus. Every day it publishes two columns of wedding announcements (before they leave, the betrothed want to get married in Pola) and four or five columns full of business announcements ('Available – half a wagon from Ancona to Terni,' 'Acct. So-And-So's office has moved, effective today, to via Caio in Vicenza,' 'Rope and nail urgently needed' repeated a hundred times like an invocation for help. 'Wanted – storage in Marghera,' 'House maid from Pola available for someone from Pola going to Spoleto'). The old blind woman that begged for coins on the steps of the Duomo has also published an announcement: she thanks everyone and says good-bye; if they leave her the votive lights, she will light them; she will learn to distinguish the tombs just as she learned to orient herself without a guide through the streets of Pola.

The 'nail crisis' is a mere illustration of the drama lived by the people of Pola and Istria, who were forced by the fury of the ethnic cleansing to abandon the land where they were born, where they had built their homes and buried their dead. Nails, stakes, boxes, and ropes were indispensable for packing the few household goods that the so-called *optanti* – that is, the Italians who refused Slavification and 'opted' for Italy – could carry with them into exile.

Among the many humilations to which Italians were subjected was a 'black list' of household objects and goods that they were absolutely forbidden to take with them to Italy. Included on this list were sewing machines, bicycles, motor vehicles, radios, and all electric appliances. Those who were leaving had to give these things to neighbours who were not leaving or to sell them for a pittance. Another brutal decree concerned the amount of money a citizen was allowed to take out of the country. Before the exodus, the amount was undetermined, except that all lire had to be changed into dinars at the rate imposed by the *Titini:* one lira to three dinars. Later, when the government allowed citizens to opt for Italy, the total amount someone could export was set at 3,000 dinars and the exchange rate was set at one-to-one. Before, if someone had 10,000 lire, he received in exchange 30,000 dinars; after the Yugoslav authorities tightened the screws, the 10,000 lire automatically became 10,000 dinars. Since no one opting for Italy could export more than 3,000 dinars, the remaining 7,000 were confiscated. No one could avoid this disgraceful theft.

At the border and at the docks, those who were leaving were forced to undergo long and meticulous searches. For hour on hour, while anguish mounted, the *drusi* and the *drugarice* (male and female comrades), standing guard at the borders opened one by one the packing crates and subjected them to endless controls; those who were fleeing stood in columns and were subjected to personal searches right down to their underwear. The militia rummaged everywhere, and many legitimate owners were robbed of a gold chain, or ring, or watch. Those who were leaving were at the complete mercy of the customs officers, without any laws to protect them or to guarantee their most basic rights.

From Our Correspondent Indro Montanelli

All of this happened in Pola in February 1947, under the eyes of the British General Robert W. De Winton, the outgoing governor of the city after the signing of the Paris Peace Treaty. The journalist Indro Montanelli, an eye witness to the exodus of Italians from Istria, wrote:

> What fills us with greater indignation is not so much the abandonment of Pola, but the manner in which it is carried out; in a constant trickle of the dead, in the constant lack of personal security, in a spider web of difficulties for our people and compliance for others: everything possible to 'de-dramatize,' everything possible to deny that there is a Pola problem. But the four who were felled yesterday, the mangled partisan agonizing in the infirmary of the *Toscana*, but this people among whom I find myself that crowds the bridges and the stowage of the ship, these mothers with their faces framed by long black kerchiefs who breast-feed their babies wrapped in red-white-and-green kerchiefs, there is no propaganda effort that can 'de-dramatize' them.

In his bitter report, Montanelli did not hesitate to argue with those who even in Italy were trying to camouflage the ethnic cleansing being conducted by the *Titini* with the carefully contrived theory that this was merely the flight from Communism of the rich bourgeoisie and the Fascists. Montanelli confesses:

> I, too, had believed, at first, that this fear belonged only to a certain class, frightened by the thought of being subjected to a given social regime and fully able to support itself even outside their own town. I was deceiving myself. Ninety-five percent of these exiles are hopelessly poor and their household furniture proclaims their poverty. Piled up inside long sheds on the Scomenzera or on the Giudecca,[1] long parades of worn out mattresses, unstable chests, broken down beds, limping chairs and tables, little bird cages with frightened canaries, little mutts tied with rope, they reveal the proletarian origin of their owners. Communism and anti-Communism have nothing to do with it. Farmers do not flee because they are anti-Communist, nor do workers or artisans, those who have nothing to lose do not flee from Communism. The only Italian left in Pola (even two madmen, one a man the other a woman, have fled) who had indicated his intention to stay, is a Communist professor who, right after the liberation, established a Italian-Slavic cultural circle playing on the card of fraternization. Yesterday he, too, asked to be put on board. Even a certain Facchetti, the Italian and Communist mayor of a small town nearby, asked to be taken away, but he did not make it in time: a bullet killed him while he was packing his bags.

The Italian Government Advises against the Exodus

One should distinguish between the exodus of over 30,000 of Pola's 34,000 inhabitants and the exodus of Italians from Zone B or from other Istrian and Dalmatian territories. The latter, as we have already mentioned, did not wait for the signing of the peace treaty before abandoning their homes and belongings. From the first days of the Slavic occupation, they fled by the thousands; but they did so one by one, risking a thousand traps and mortal dangers with every means at their disposal and paying out of their own pocket anyone who might be able to transport them to Italy. 'They flee from their own city,' reported the

---

1 Giudecca and Scomenzera are two important commercial canals in Venice. The 'Stazione marittima,' the passenger port of Venice, is on the north shore of the Canal della Giudecca; the Canal di Scomenzera runs parallel to, and immediately east of the basin of the 'Marittima' and joins the Canal della Giudecca to the Canal Grande (translator's note).

secretary of the Rovigno National Liberation Committee in September 1945, 'abandoning everything, by night, across the woods or across the sea on small boats, even before knowing to which nation their city will be assigned.'

The scenes that took place at border crossings, or along the coastal landings of the Veneto, the Romagna, and the Marche, were not very different from the ones seen fifty years later at the borders of Albania or along the coast of Puglia.[2] The difference is that back then, there was no television to document them. Unfortunately, nor were there any suitable refugee centres to house them.

In spite of the severe episodes of ethnic cleansing, which could not have been missed by the Italian authorities, the Italian government tried in every possible way to discourage the exodus. It feared that the flight of the Italians and the influx of Slavic immigrants from the Yugoslav interior would change the ethnic composition of the area and thereby harm Italian claims on Venezia Giulia during the negotiations at the peace conference. In a private letter to Prime Minister Ivanoe Bonomi, the Italian foreign minister, Alcide De Gasperi, had even proposed (certainly in good faith) that about 120,000 Italians from the region – refugees, soldiers, and ex-deportees to Germany – currently housed as best could be in refugee centres, should be helped to return to their homes, perhaps with the encouragement of subsidies.

The Italian Communist Party also obstructed the exodus, but for completely different reasons. Officially, it did so because, as Togliatti said, 'it could not see the need' for a mass escape from friendly Yugoslavia. In reality, it feared the negative repercussions the exodus would have on public perceptions of Communism.

Italians living in Zone B were able to resist longer the desire to flee, deluding themselves with the hope that the peace conference would not assign the Free Territory of Trieste to Yugoslavia. But in July 1946, when the British foreign minister, Ernest Bevin, announced in the Commons that the Allies were leaning toward the 'French line,' panic broke out. Nearly all Italians in the zone requested expatriation; meanwhile, the Yugoslav authorities took measures to regulate the exodus to their advantage. For example, everything possible was done to hold back technicians and specialized workers through enticements and promises

2 In the 1990s Puglia, the Italian region directly across the Adriatic from Albania, bore the brunt of the illegal immigration of Albanian refugees fleeing from the disastrous situation in their homeland and in the Balkans generally (translator's note).

of assured employment. At the same time, the 'price' that voluntary exiles would have to pay was raised. For example, all those who opted for Italy automatically lost their ration cards and jobs. Anyone who owned land lost every right of ownership, but was obligated, in the meantime, to pay taxes on that land for the entire year. Keeping in mind that it would take months for a request to be processed and for permission to expatriate to be granted, this meant that many *optanti* faced poverty and hunger. Another disposition allowed the authorities to expel from Zone B the relatives of anyone deemed to be a Fascist. The same regulation touched the relatives of anyone who had already expatriated. Everyone was allowed to take along hand baggage; the rest was expropriated.

The Pola National Liberation Committee Rebels against De Gasperi

The exodus of Italians from Pola began later and, unlike the one from Zone B, it was sudden and massive. As we mentioned earlier, Pola was part of Zone A, administered by the Allies, and represented a sort of little 'happy island' in the heart of Slavicized Istria. Because of its privileged position, many Italians from neighbouring towns had flocked to it when fleeing persecution at the hands of the Yugoslav authorities. The suddenly larger population and the city's isolation – it could be provisioned only by sea – had created enormous problems. The cost of living had increased astronomically, and the black market was everywhere. Even so, the sense of security sustained by the presence of Allied soldiers made the situation bearable.

Even toward the end of 1946, there was in the city a certain optimism, reinforced by rumours that the Allies had no intention of ceding this important naval base to Tito. As a result, all the requests advanced by the Pola National Liberation Committee that a plan be set in place for a possible evacuation of the city were ignored by the government in Rome, because the ceding of Pola to Yugoslavia was considered improbable, and also because an early exodus might have negative repercussions for Italy at the peace conference then underway in Paris.

Toward the end of December 1946, everything indicated that the Allies were about to adopt the 'French line,' which stipulated (among other things) the automatic transfer of Pola to Yugoslav sovereignty. Yet even at this point, the Italian government continued to waste precious time. Out of ignorance of the actual situation, or because of naked political opportunism, Rome continued to discourage an exodus. For example, Alcide De Gasperi, now Italy's prime minister, repeatedly asked the representatives of Pola to do everything possible to prevent an exodus. According to him, it was in the national interest for Italians to remain in Pola. If they remained, representing as they did nearly 100 per cent of the population, the Italian government would have the leverage to 'recover' the city at a later date. If the Italian population left and was replaced by Slavic immigrants, Italy would definitively lose its rights to the city.

This rationale perhaps would have had some validity had the border dispute been between two democratic countries. But the citizens of Pola had already suffered under Yugoslav domination for forty-five days, and they remembered those days well; under no circumstances did they want to go through that terrible experience again. So when the Pola delegates returned from Rome with the news that the Italian government was discounting the need for an exodus, the entire city rebelled. Shock and anger were everywhere. The wave of protest struck even at the prime minister, who was accused of cynicism or of not understanding the situation and the impending danger.

To be fair, De Gasperi was facing a complex and delicate situation. He was head of the government, so it was his duty to do all he could to safeguard Italy's rights to Pola. At the same time, he was a politician, and the Secretary of the Italian Communist Party, Palmiro Togliatti, was attacking him violently, accusing him publicly of being the 'instigator' of an unnecessary exodus. Finally, he was a human being, and he could not summon the strength to call for an entire population to leap into the unknown, in the dead of winter, toward an Italy destroyed by war and unable to receive them adequately.

This was why, at the end of December, when it was announced that on 10 February 1947, Pola would pass from Allied to Yugoslav control, the Pola National Liberation Committee boldly presented the government in Rome with a *fait accompli* by declaring that the exodus from the city was underway. At that point, every family had to choose its fate.

Two Voices from the Silence

'There are things that happen and one does not really know why,' say Anna Maria Mori and Nelida Milani in *Bora*, a beautiful and moving book they have written together. Anna Maria and Nelida are two 'girls of '47' from Pola. The exodus has divided them and made them foreigners to each other. Their book explains the Julian drama better than any essay could:

Events happen, that's it, and we are in them. What can we change? A type of anguish hangs in the air and penetrates to the bottom of our heart. From the hills silvery with olive trees and from the towns, from the woods and the streets, from the beaches of rocks jutting out to sea, from the vineyards growing in stone fortresses, hundreds of thousands of figures and voices come in procession. They follow one another in debates, discussions, visits by international commissions, conflicting parades, spit and invective, speeches from podiums, Communist preaching – head thrown back, fist on the table like a hammer – according to whom the only truth is theirs, articulated, yelled, angrily shouted out. And everything on the heads of the people, poor them, as if a trial was in progress for crimes reaching back into history, primeval, at fault for having been born under a wrong star.

Among the forewarned there were those who felt *imbiliati* [infuriated] against De Gasperi, those broken down by pain, those who started to think when they were not able to find their happiness in the first five-year plan, those who spoke about this and that in the grips of tantrums of self-compassion or on the edge of desperation, those who would later commit suicide because they did not know how to choose between a sudden departure and a slow impoverished ruin, those who immediately put their head in the noose and tightened it around their neck slowly and carefully as if it were their Sunday tie, those who cried because they had already suffered great damage, they had lost everything in the bombings and they had not yet fixed the damage, so they defended themselves against the fury of winter with anything they could get their hands on, tables, wooden beams, plugs, doors, stolen from military batteries and from work sites, those who drowned in the tears they shed, those who purchased evenings in front of the heavy drinking glass of the tavern, those who were happy and hugged everyone calling everyone 'comrade,' those who could not swallow the Slav, they tried but could not do it, sold their furniture for a couple of coins, did not eat any more and moved house with a tomb dug inside their head, those who found the matter scandalous and those who found it natural and just, those who put into practice the usual fireplace philosophy 'hey kids, mouth shut, let's first see which way the wind will blow' in a kind of acquiescence, a willingness to adapt, to accept and even to try somehow to reap some benefit from it, those who used strong and primordial antidotes such as irony, grains of folly, a mocking disposition crowned with a gesture that was so much in vogue then, complete with slap on the butt and the exclamation '*ciana!*,'[3] those who turned it into a joke because no one had the power to help out in that difficult situation, and so they laughed because they fervently believed in 'humour,' and they sang under their breath '*avanti popolo, è giunta l'ora, chi non lavora, non mangerà*'[4] and, when they could bear it no longer, they chose departure with no return.

They Even Take the Dead Away

While Rome kept delaying, offices for the evacuation were opened in Pola, refugee certificates were distributed, and some sail ships were hired for carting away household goods. According to the organizers' regulations, these goods had to be piled along the docks, from which they would be shipped to Italy ahead of their rightful owners. The entire city soon turned into an immense carpenter shop. Every house echoed with hammer blows. Planks, boxes, and cartons became precious packing materials. Nails were especially scarce, and were rationed (300 grams per family). Since there were no restrictions such as those imposed by the Yugoslavs in Zone B, the people of Pola hoped to take all their belongings with them. Many went to the cemetery to exhume their dead, intending to take away their bones. Nearly everyone took a piece of stone from the ancient Roman Arena as a memento of their city. Even the body of the First World War hero Nazario Sauro was packed for transfer to Venice.

All of this was happening during the Christmas holidays. This was certainly the saddest Christmas ever for the people of Pola. Having piled up their household goods along the docks, having ceased all work, having exhausted every chance of acquiring food, they camped out in their empty houses, waiting to board the ships the Italian government should have sent. Even the weather lashed out against those who

---

3 In Tuscan, *ciana* is a woman of ill repute. However, according to the dictionaries and the Istriani I have consulted, the word is not used in Istria and does not exist in any local dialect. A more likely exclamation that might have been used by Istriani might have been *ciapa* ('take this!'), generally used with some sort of a gesture, obscene or otherwise (translator's note).

4 'Forward, people! The time has come, those who won't work, won't get to eat'; a parody on the Italian Communist marching song 'Avanti popolo, alla riscossa, bandiera rossa trionferà!' 'Forward, people! On to revolt, the red flag will triumph!' (translator's note).

were leaving. The transport of things and people was carried out under constant snow and rain, which disintegrated many of the piles of household goods stacked along the docks (figs. 9–10).

In their beautiful book, Nelida tells Anna Maria:

I remember the sound of the hammers hitting on the nails, the truck that carried my aunt Regina's bedroom furniture to the coal dock, *molo Carbon*, moving between buildings mortally pale with fear, and all the packing getting soaked in the snow and the rain. The big ship left twice every month, from its chimneys the smoke rose to the sky like incense and instilled into our spirit the subtle torment of uncertainty and the shadow of unease; everyone felt ever more depressed by the air of calamity that hovered on friends as they met on the street.

In due time the *Toscana* had guzzled all the people of Pola: the upper class families, many professionals, the pharmacist, the officer who married the Czechoslovak woman, the dentist who married the Hungarian, the singer who married the Slovenian, the English teacher who married the Italian, the widow of a Jew, the beautiful Vanda who received the American soldiers, the man who used to bum American cigarettes, the drunkard who, warm with the grappa in his body, would melt the snow wherever he fell, the old accordion player with his little mutt, the Antoni sisters who boarded even their dying father, even though they could not reasonably think the old man could come back as they hoped they would do, nor could he have reached the destination they had in mind. Even the parish priest of Gallesano left, dragging behind him a large box of his most beloved texts, Saint Augustine, Saint Theresa, and announcing the end of the world for the following Sunday. Hundreds of Gallesani believed him. But when they saw that nothing had happened they did not get mad, as one might have thought. They just figured the priest had miscalculated and most of them did not stop believing in him. The world of a thousand professions left, the worker and the artisan, the farmer and the cigarette woman, the gardener, the tinsmith, the carter, the chair mender, the barrel maker, the baker, the bricklayer, the veterinary: the workers from the factory left, the smelters, the smiths, the mechanics of the *K. und K. Marine Arsenal*,[5] the mechanics and the lathe operators from Scoglio Ulivi, the carpenters and the cobblers, the plumber, the seamstress, the pasta maker, the barber, the shop boys, the fishermen who

---

5 'The Royal and Imperial Marine Arsenal,' established under Austrian rule the previous century (translator's note).

smelled of salt and oysters and seaweed, the small artisans of every thing, from wine to bricks, from tallow to glass, from hats to ribbons, from pastries to salami, from boats to books, from lyric opera to newspapers. The fathers of the partisan boys left, and then also the ex-partisans. They had sought in vain to face up to an incomprehensible civilization. What had they done to deserve that world where they felt they had no possibility to live a full life, a truly human life? For us who were staying, it was the beginning of a new era. Afterwards, in fact, things would never be the same, nor easy.

'Fascist' Istrians Unwanted Guests

The spontaneous exodus of all the people of Pola, with some rare exceptions, without distinction of class or political affiliation, had a profound effect on Italian public opinion. The Communist press was seriously embarrassed. It was becoming ever more difficult to claim that those emaciated masses of refugees desperately piling up in the refugee camps consisted of 'Fascists' and 'enemies of the people.' Nonetheless, the party's political agitators, its agit-prop specialists, did not tone down their baffling propaganda. Dark events took place in those days that are better forgotten. In Venice, the first refugees disembarking from the *Toscana* – including many partisans from the 'Budicin' battalion, which had fought alongside the Slavs – were met by a hostile demonstration. A volley of jeers was reserved for the body of Nazario Sauro.

In Bologna, where a Pontifical Assistance Office was operating, the incredible happened: the Communist railwaymen threatened to go on strike if a train of refugees coming from Ancona entered the station. The convoy, with its desperate human cargo, was sent back and redirected toward La Spezia, on the other side of the Italian peninsula. There, the refugees were housed in the Italian Royal Navy barracks. Subsequently, they were lodged in apartments made available to them by the municipal government.

The story of Pola is intimately tied to that of the navy, which had turned the city into an efficient stronghold, a forge of men accustomed to the harsh travails of life at sea. This quality bound Pola spiritually and economically to other navy cities such as La Spezia, Livorno, and Taranto, where many of the refugees had relatives, friends, colleagues, and where they found, more than anywhere else, a warm welcome.

The episodes of incivility were limited and localized; that said, Istrian refugees as a whole were not received in Italy with any great effusions of solidarity. Times were very difficult, and people were struggling with their own personal survival problems. The heavy propaganda aimed at safeguarding the image of Communism was contributing to the cool welcome these unwanted guests were receiving.

An article by Palmiro Togliatti, published in *L'Unità* on 2 February 1947, worsened the situation and gave rise to debates, doubts, and uncertainties. 'Why evacuate Pola?' asked the Secretary of the Italian Communist Party. He accused the government (of which he himself was a member) of carrying out a policy that, regarding the Italianness of Pola, constituted 'a sacrifice that is carried out gratuitously, perhaps in spite, but without having anyone evaluate coldly and with a national view the extent, the meaning, the consequences.' He then affirmed that 'among the Italians that encourage it there are, without a doubt, people acting in good faith, but there are also, without a doubt, people who have an interest in keeping alive down there a hotbed of discord.'

In the meantime, the government in Rome was being swamped with complaints and appeals, some of them from highly influential people. The Italian consul Justo Giusti Del Giardino was urging that ships be sent because 'it is unthinkable that the Italians of Pola could remain under Tito's regime, because martyrdom is not the goal of the masses.' For his part, the Bishop of Pola, Monsignor Radossi, sent a telegram directly to Prime Minister De Gasperi stating that 'people are sleeping on the bare floor. Furniture rots on the docks for lack of transportation. Food supplies may fail. I beg you to take urgent action. No point waiting. You must act. Understand it once and for all and believe it, *otherwise, you come here and we shall leave.'*

Finally, on 27 January, the Italian government decided to intervene. The exodus of the people of Pola began at the beginning of February. Most exiles left the city on the *Toscana*, but smaller vessels were also used, such as the motor launches *Montecucco*, *Messina*, *Pola*, and *Grado*.

The exodus echoed loudly around the world. Dozens of special correspondents from various countries, as well as newsreels, movingly described the drama of the people of Pola, which at the time could be compared only to the flight of German populations from regions occupied by the Red Army.

By 20 March, after the *Toscana* had carried out its tenth and last voyage, the city was practically deserted. But only for a brief time: new inhabitants rushed in from the periphery and the suburbs to take over the houses, which their owners had left vacant, the doors wide open and often with a tricolour at the window.

On Board the *Toscana*

In their moving diary, Anna Maria recalls the voyage for Nelida:

We boarded at evening, again grey, rain, frost, silence, shawls, umbrellas. We go down to the stowage. Someone, so as not to think and not to talk, pulls out a deck of cards and a bottle of wine. Thoughts and pain are too great: there's need for alcohol to keep them quiet. And at night, packed like sardines in a can, in three rows of couchettes one above the other, hundreds of men, women, and children make believe they are asleep and make believe they are not crying, all equal in the same pain and in the same fear, they return unequal again: those above, drunk, piss on each other and water those below who, however, do not utter a word, they just open their umbrellas. At night, on route to Venice, anyone who would have looked into the great black belly of the *Toscana* would have seen in the couchettes on the first level a row of umbrellas, also black: if we must resign ourselves to the rain God sends on poor unfortunates, why should we not resign ourselves to the rain that comes from human beings? ...

'Daddy, when we came away, leaving that house that was ours, what did you do? Did you close the door and throw away the key without looking back?'

'I gave the keys to those who had been sent there to take possession of the house. And, think about it, I also left them a long list of the things they would have to do and not do, and I urged them to write me to keep me informed. They seemed like good people, but they never wrote to me. The house was still mine, nominally, but the Yugoslav government requisitioned the rent money in order to recover the maintenance costs. When we returned to Pola after five years, we discovered that the relationship between the government's maintenance costs and the intake from the rents for the purpose of keeping up the house was very unbalanced: we owed the Yugoslav government I don't know how many dinars for repairs to the window shutters ... Conclusion: in a short while the villa will be nationalized.'

'From the Bog of Italy a Flower Is Born'

On the morning of 10 February 1947, Brigadier General Robert W. De Winton, commander of the British garrison in Pola, left his lodgings early. A demanding day was ahead of him. At the same hour, in Paris, the ceremony of the signing of the peace treaty by the Italian delegates would be taking place. His task was to carry out the most delicate of the clauses of that treaty: the handing over of the enclave of Pola to the Yugoslav military authorities.

That morning was very cold. A freezing *bora* swept the streets of a city that seemed to have dismantled itself. The lights in the bars were out, the stop blinds were down, groups of people were struggling and swearing around carts and wheelbarrows full of household goods. For about twenty months, the inhabitants, reassured by the presence of Allied soldiers, had basked in the illusion that they might escape the bitter destiny that had touched other Italians in the region. But now all their dreams had collapsed, and they had to come to terms with reality.

At the express wish of the Yugoslav military command, the transfer of power over the city of Pola was to take place simultaneously with the signing of the treaty. For the occasion, the British garrison had lined up in front of their headquarters. As soon as General De Winton arrived, he was invited to review it. The ceremony took place under the rain, in front of a few curious onlookers, from whom there rose some disapproving mutterings and a few hostile cries: the people of Pola felt abandoned and betrayed by their protectors.

De Winton was advancing toward the unit drawn up on the square when a young woman came out of the small group of on-lookers and approached him. It was a matter of seconds: she pulled a pistol from her purse and fired repeatedly without uttering a word. Three bullets struck the general in the heart and he died instantly. A fourth bullet wounded a soldier who tried to protect him.

Having carried out the crime, the young woman stood immobile, as if in a trance. Meekly, she allowed herself to be restrained by the soldiers who had fallen on her.

The Allied authorities considered the delicacy of the moment and for some days maintained absolute silence regarding this astonishing event. The most outlandish rumours about it were allowed to circulate: it was a crime of passion, an individual act of hysteria, a Fascist or a Yugoslav provocation, and so on. Only later, thanks to a scoop by Indro Montanelli, who was in Pola as a correspondent for *Corriere della Sera*, was it possible to determine what really motivated the assassin. The soldiers had discovered in her pocket a written confession. In it after a rhetorical preamble on the Italianness of Istria and on the blood shed by Italian martyrs, she wrote: 'I rebel, with the firm intention of killing the man who is unfortunate enough to represent the Four Great Powers that, at the Conference in Paris, in violation of justice, against humanity, and against political wisdom, have decided to tear out once again from the maternal womb the lands most sacred to Italy, condemning them either to the experiments of a new Danzig or, with a chilling sensibility and complicity, to the Yugoslav yoke that, for our indomitable Italian people, is synonymous with death in the *foibe*, with deportation, with exile.'

The assassin had acted alone and on her own initiative. Her name was Maria Pasquinelli (fig. 6). She was born in Florence in 1913 and lived for some time in Bergamo, where she graduated as an elementary schoolteacher and, subsequently, in pedagogy. A fervent Fascist, she attended the 'school of Fascist ideology' in Rome. In 1940, she enrolled as a Red Cross volunteer with the Italian troops in North Africa. Motivated by deep and somewhat excessive love for the Motherland, she now dedicated herself to what she considered her mission, rejecting family and sentimental ties. On the Libyan front, as she would recount in one of her memoirs, she noticed 'the insufficient participation in the struggle of those who had preached it,' not to mention the low morale of the troops who were 'not enlightened by any ideal.' Her fanaticism often led her to make bizarre gestures. In November 1941, she left the hospital at El Abiar, where she was working, and reached the front dressed as a soldier, her head shaven and carrying false identity papers. When she was discovered, she was returned to her superiors, who repatriated her.

In January 1942, she asked to be sent as a teacher to Dalmatia. For some time, she taught Italian in the schools in Spalato. After 8 September and the massacres of Italians carried out in Dalmatia and Istria, she dedicated herself to the recovery of the bodies of Italian soldiers killed by the Slavs and to recording the atrocities of the *foibe*. In Spalato, she located a mass grave containing the bodies of two hundred soldiers from the Bergamo Division and took an active part in recovering the bodies of hundreds of victims of the *foibe*.

She moved to Trieste and began to overwhelm the authorities of the Italian Social Republic with memoranda and denunciations. She tried to establish contact with the Tenth Mas and with the Italian partisans of the Franchi and Osoppo brigades, with the intention of setting up an organization for the defence of the Italianness of the region. As a result of these activities, the Germans arrested her and threatened her with deportation. She was saved by the personal intervention of Junio Valerio Borghese, commander of the Tenth Mas.

Maria Pasquinelli was described by those who knew her as excitable and impetuous, as well as a fierce debater. So it is not surprising that she experienced a sort of psychic trauma when she learned that the four great powers had abandoned Pola and Istria to their fate. She assassinated General De Winton in order to call the world's attention to the sufferings of Italians in Istria. In fact, the assassination did make news worldwide, raising many questions. It also led to some soul searching among Italians. The Communist press dismissed the event as a 'Fascist regurgitation.' But the world press, for its part, expressed compassion and sympathy for the young Italian woman. The dispatch from Associated Press is worth noting. Michael Goldsmith, its correspondent in Pola, wrote: 'There are many guilty parties. The Italian population of Pola finds no-one who understands their feelings. The Rome government is absent, the Slavs are declared enemies waiting to enter the city and occupy their houses, the Allies are cold and extremely wary. The inhabitants of Pola blame these, and especially the British, for not having kept their promises, for having abandoned them.'

Maria Pasquinelli was tried two months after the event by the Allied Military Court in Trieste. The trial unfolded without incidents or commotions. The accused confessed her guilt and explained why she had committed the crime. The presiding officer, Chapman, had the courtroom cleared only once. This happened with the defending lawyer, Giannini, invited by the presiding judge to adhere to the procedures established by the Allied court, answered: 'Before all else, Your Honour, I consider myself to be an Italian defending an Italian.' The statement sparked applause among the public and cries of 'Long live Italy.' At that point, the court room was cleared.

On 10 April, the Allied court sentenced Maria Pasquinelli to death. The accused remained silent, the public cursed under its breath, and women in the courtroom burst into tears. The following day, Trieste was flooded by a rain of tricolour flyers bearing these words: 'From the bog of Italy a flower is born: Maria Pasquinelli.'

The death sentence was later commuted to life imprisonment, and Maria Pasquinelli was transferred to the penitentiary in Perugia. Set free in 1964, she has never granted an interview and has tried to be forgotten. She now lives in Bergamo.

The 'Red Counter-Exodus'

While hundreds of thousands of Italians abandoned their homes to flee Communism and Slavification, other Italians – albeit in much smaller numbers – chose to head in the opposite direction, driven by a utopian faith in socialism. Little has been said in past decades about this counter-exodus, which came to a much more tragic conclusion than the bitter and dramatic exodus of the Istrian refugees. This chapter of Julian history was destined to remain sealed forever in the archives of the Italian Communist Party. Only after the fall of the Berlin Wall and the collapse of Communism did some survivors, feeling themselves liberated from party discipline, begin to speak about it.

The void left in the Istrian countryside by the forced exodus of the Italian population had been filled easily by an influx of Slovenian and Croatian farmers brought in from the Yugoslav interior. The same approach was impossible for the cities, and especially for the once efficient and busy shipyards of Pola and Fiume. In spite of enticements and promises from the authorities, the Italian workers, with few exceptions, preferred exile. It was impossible to repopulate the shipyards, as had been done with the countryside, because of the complete lack of qualified labour in Yugoslavia. Yet it was vital for the Belgrade government to get the country's industrial production moving. To address this problem, the Slavic theorists of ethnic cleansing were forced to re-evaluate their beliefs and to ask for help from their Italian 'comrades.'

'Operation Counter-Exodus,' planned in absolute secrecy, was the product of an agreement between the leaders of Yugoslav and Italian communism. Pietro Secchia, the Vice-Secretary of the Italian Communist Party, personally arranged matters on the Italian side. The operation involved the clandestine transfer to Yugoslavia of Italian volunteers, recruited from the shipyards of Monfalcone and from factories in Gorizia, Trieste, and Friuli. Their duty would be to help 'build socialism' in Yugoslavia (as they used to put it in those days). Put simply, they were to teach the Yugoslavs how to operate the shipyards they had confiscated from the Italians.

This unique exodus-in-reverse also had a political purpose. The presence of Italian workers in the yards and factories of Pola and Fiume would allow the Communist press to claim that not all Italians, but only the 'Fascists,' had chosen exile.

The Italo-Slovenian Anti-Fascist Union organized the counter-exodus in secrecy, but with great effort on the part of its various sections. The Italian volunteers numbered about two thousand. They and their families were sent to Yugoslavia in groups. They were all committed Communists. Many had fought in Yugoslav units during the partisan war. Animated by a spirit that lept over national boundaries, they were proud to be able to participate in the building of socialism in a country that had liberated itself from Nazism on its own and that had built its national unity on the principle of the brotherhood of the people. They were animated as well by pride in being part of the mythical 'proletarian aristocracy,' which Lenin had described as the 'diamond point' of the proletarian revolution.

The Monfalconesi, as they would generally be known, began arriving in Yugoslavia toward the middle of 1947, while the exodus of Italians from Istria was still in full swing. No one noticed their counter-exodus, or at least, it was not documented in the press. The new arrivals were destined mainly for the industries and the Arsenal in Fiume and for the shipyards in Pola. Others were distributed throughout various locations in the heart of Yugoslavia, where the need for skilled labour was strongest. Wherever they arrived, they were welcomed with dignity and adequately billeted with local families. Their salaries were decent, and their dwellings were chosen from among the best available in the city that hosted them. They were also allowed complete autonomy for political organization. All were members of the Italian Communist Party and were permitted to reconstitute their cells and sections. The charismatic leaders of the Monfalconesi were three workers: Ferdinando Marega, who had been political commissar in an Italo-Slovenian brigade; Angelo Comar, also an ex-partisan; and Sergio Mori, a young elementary schoolteacher from La Spezia, who worked as a machine operator.

For the first few months, everything went smoothly. Except for some incidents of chauvinism on the part of the Yugoslavs and the defection of a few Italians, who decided to return home after realizing their expectations would not be met, there were no incidents worth noting. The Monfalconesi worked hard and with enthusiasm. They carried out intense political activity, and they maintained close ties with the federation of the Italian Communist Party in Trieste. With their status as indispensable experts and through their membership in the strongest Communist party in the West, they knew how to inspire respect. When something was not right in the factory, they did not hesitate to organize some form of protest. On one occasion, they even went on strike – the first strike in the history of Communist Yugoslavia. Riccardo Bellobarbich, a Monfalconese who survived that terrible experience, recounts: 'It was not for political reasons, but because of the red pepper ... Their overly spicy food was not to our liking. We protested in vain and in the end we decided to stop working. This was unheard of, for the Yugoslavs. The other workers looked at us in amazement, as if we were Martians. But in the end we won, and the cooks in the dining halls adapted themselves to our wishes.'

The real problems began in 1948, with the break between Tito and Stalin, after Yugoslavia refused to adhere to the Cominform, the organ Stalin had created to impose obedience to the Soviet Union on all other Communist parties. For the Monfalconesi, who were die-hard Stalinists and members of the Italian Communist Party (whose undisputed leader, Palmiro Togliatti, was one of the first to sign the resolution that 'excommunicated' Tito), this was traumatic. They were animated by blind and absolute faith in the Soviet Union; thus, to rebel against Stalin's will was, for them, worse than a sacrilege. They could not believe their ears. Had not Milovan Gilas – at that time Tito's right-hand man and a theorist of Marxism, affirmed that 'without Stalin even the sun would not shine as it does'? Yet now, Tito was daring to disobey the great and beloved leader of all workers, deserting the fight for socialism and repudiating that faith which had given them the strength to fight fearlessly against Fascism and to withstand both prison and torture. For the Monfalconesi, all of this was unacceptable.

The Monfalconese 'Fifth Column'

The first to take action were the Italian workers in the shipyards in Fiume and Pola. Supplied through secret channels by the Communist Party of the Free Territory of Trieste, headed by Vittorio Vidali, and by the Italian Communist Party of Palmiro Togliatti, the Monfalconesi constituted for some time a Cominformist 'fifth column,' whose duty was to bring Yugoslavia back into the Soviet orbit and to free it from Tito's 'gang,' who according to the Communist press had become the 'lackeys of imperialism.' For some time they were not bothered. Tito's regime was not yet ready to deal with the supporters of the Cominform. Besides, the two thousand and more Monfalconesi amounted to a strong political force with plenty of influence among those Yugoslav Communists who had not yet aligned themselves with the new course.

For some time, Ferdinando Marega, Angelo Comar, and Sergio Mori – the recognized leaders of the Cominform group – were left free to organize meetings and maintain contacts with the Trieste federation. However, the political police did not let them out of their sight. After some time, the Yugoslav leaders responded; in an effort to clarify matters, they convened the Monfalconesi at the Partizan Theatre in Fiume. Just over two hundred people were expected, but the theatre, which could seat 1,500, turned out to be too small for all those who attended. Hour after hour, the leaders from Zagreb struggled to explain the position taken by the Yugoslav Communist Party and to fight against the 'libels of the Cominform.' A waste of energy: their speeches were interrupted by rumblings of protest and overwhelmed with whistling. Every so often, a cry would rise up from the audience: 'Long live comrade Stalin.' This would be followed by thunderous applause. The situation continued to degenerate until Ferdinando Marega stood up and declared: 'This place is not for us. Let's leave!' He headed for the exit, followed by all of those present, who raised cheers in praise of Stalin, Togliatti, and the Soviet Union. On the street, the Italian Cominformists formed a dense procession that marched down the Corso singing the 'International.' This was the first demonstration ever held against the Communist rulers in the name of Communism.

Naturally, the Yugoslavs could not tolerate this. Toward the end of 1948, the OZNA, the notorious Yugoslav political police, sprang into action. It rounded up Monfalconesi and shipped them to prison camps in the interior or to island prisons. Only Ferdinando Marega was able to escape capture. After operating clandestinely for some time, he was able to return to Italy. When he arrived, he immediately informed the party of what was happening in Yugoslavia. He told of persecutions, tortures, deportations, and 'gulags' where many comrades who had not wanted to renounce the faith had been locked up. But he was not heard. In fact, as all other Monfalconesi who survived the Yugoslav inferno know, he was invited to keep silent so as 'not to undermine the party.' At that time, the Communist press was allowed to defame Tito with every possible libel, but it was not allowed to mention the existence of Yugoslav gulags; the party did not want to draw attention to those much more numerous gulags that had long existed in the Soviet Union. Thus, the Italian Communist Party abandoned the Monfalconesi to their tragic fate.

The Cries from the Silence

'I was only six years old then, but the memory of that time is alive in me and those dramatic images still weigh like a frightening shadow on my conscience as a man and as a Communist.' These are the words of Armido Campo, the son of Ribella and a nephew of Vinicio Fontanot, the famous leader of the Garibaldi-Natisone Brigade. He now lives in La Spezia. Fifty years after the event, he decided to break the silence his family had imposed on itself out of party discipline. Armido recounted:

We were all hard-core Communists. My mother, Ribella, widow of a man deported to Germany, had remarried with Sergio Mori, my second father, who at that time was among the leaders of the Italian Communist Party. We left Monfalcone at the beginning of 1947 in order to go live in Yugoslavia, inside real Communism, from which the Italians of Istria were fleeing en masse. After the break between Tito and Stalin, my family was deported to Zenica, in Bosnia. There were other families of Monfalconesi with us: the Battilana, the Bressan, the Comar, the Babuder, the Gratton, and Elsa Fontanot. In that village we came in touch with the German prisoners condemned to forced labour. I remember my mother's and my grandmother Lisa's pity who, forgetting that the Nazi had killed their husbands, would bring bowls of soup to those prisoners stuck deep in the snow. We, too, to tell the truth, lived like prisoners, but we were not chained like the Germans. We stayed there for more than a year, completely forgotten by the Italian Communist Party, which could not have been ignorant of what was happening. Vittorio Vidali, certainly, knew everything. But no one did anything for us. Because of this, one day Sergio Mori decided to escape from Zenica and was able to reach Zagreb, where he contacted the Italian consul. A short time later, thanks to the intervention of the Italian government, we were freed, we returned to Italy, but we fell from the frying pan into the fire ... Our homes in Monfalcone had been assigned to the refugees from Istria, and our jobs as well. They considered us lepers ... So Sergio decided to return to La Spezia, his native city. Some time after, he wrote to us: come, everyone, I have found a job at the Motosi shipyard. And we left ... When we arrived they told us that Sergio had died when he fell in the stowage. He was not yet thirty years old.

In the Hell of Isola Calva

Riccardo Bellobarbich was also a diehard Communist. A worker qualified as an aeronautical fitter, he, too, left Monfalcone in order to move to the Socialist country next door, where he paid dearly for his Stalinism. He was thirty-three years old when, in January 1947, he was assigned to the Icarus aeronautical factory in Zemun, near Belgrade. Riccardo recounted:

Everything went smoothly until Tito's schism exploded. They arrested me because I had organized a collection for our comrades deported to Bosnia and I was condemned to twenty-eight months of 'socially useful work' on the island of Sveti Grgur, San Gregorio. In reality, I was condemned to forced labour. It was a very confused time: I remember that, some months after, even the judge who had sentenced me and the lawyer for the prosecution from my trial were also interned with me. Detention was meant to foster 'repentance.' At the head of each hut there was a *kapò*, a 'repentant,' and every day there were meetings with strict interrogations. They wanted to know everything about our external relations with comrades and if we did not talk they beat us. Some inmates even committed suicide, other denounced relatives and family members. It was winter and I was subjected to ten days of isolation with food at half rations and without heavy clothing. At the end of the twenty-eight months, the internal 'tribunal' of *kapò* determined that I was not yet 'repentant' and so they sent me to Goli Otok, Isola Calva, the Bald Island, for the last phase of my re-education. We had to break stones using other stones. Those who stopped had to be beaten by their fellows and those who did not beat him were also beaten. I spent another six months on Goli Otok, then I was freed. I returned to Fiume: I wanted to return to Italy, but I had no money, work, or passport. This is when the police attempts to force me to become an informer began. I managed to let them think I had. I took up my old job again until they granted me a permit to return to Italy. This was 1952.

Goli Otok, Isola Calva, Bald Island. In today's tourist flyers it is described as follows: 'Island of peace, surrounded by an extremely clean sea, an immaculate location, immersed in silence, an island of absolute freedom.' Yet until not so many years ago, instead, Goli Otok was the last circle of Communist hell. Milovan Gilas, who visited it, called it 'our most shameful stain.' Situated in the Gulf of Quarnero, formed by rocks of a blinding whiteness, Bald Island was the worst of the many Yugoslav camps where hundreds of Monfalconesi, and many other prisoners, ended up. Completely uninhabited, it had been transformed into a type of Devil's Island by the notorious Yugoslav Minister of the Interior, Aleksandar Ranković. Its existence was revealed only a few years ago, thanks to the testimony of the journalist Giacomo Scotti, to an autobiographical account by Livio Zanini, and to the stories of a few of its survivors.

Goli Otok was just as bad as the Nazi prison camps and the Soviet gulags. Isolation, hunger, beatings, head in the toilet, exposure to freezing temperatures, tortures of all kinds were the order of the day. And everything kept fanatically strict time to the chorus in praise of Tito and the party – 'Tito-Partija! Tito-Partija!' – which the prisoners had to shout while they worked.

The most perverse torture was the 'repentance.' To demonstrate that he had repented, the prisoner had to beat savagely those of his fellow inmates who were slow in repentance. Those who refused ended up in *boikot* – that is, in total isolation and exposed to anyone's violence. Virgilio Giacomini, an Italian who stayed on Goli Otok until 1953 and who underwent the harsh experience of the *boikot*, recounted:

> When we were boycotted we also wore another sign of distinction besides the black shirt [which was imposed on those who were deported to Goli Otok for a second time (author's note)]: red striped pants, like the Carabinieri. Those of us in black shirt and red-striped pants were the super-boycotted. This meant that anyone could beat us at any time, without any reason, and without having to answer to anyone. Many, in fact, beat us, especially the Montenegrins, in order to show that they were faithful to their duties and completely re-educated. I wore the black shirts for more than a hundred days until Minister Ranković arrived on Goli Otok. I, too, saw him, he passed near our group. After his visit they took off our black shirts and a softer system began to make its inroads. There were no more beatings, except in extreme cases. They could mistreat us only verbally, spit in our faces and carry out other tyrannical acts against us.

The Families Answer, the Party Does Not

In 1953, after Stalin's death and the de-Stalinization process brought about by Nikita Khrushchev, the many Monfalconesi detained in the prison camps began to hope for liberation. About half of them would in fact benefit from an amnesty at the end of that year. But they also felt disillusioned. The detained Cominformists now lacked both an adversary to confront and a political cause to sustain them in their imprisonment. They were not yet aware that they had fought for nothing, and they were beginning to doubt the Italian Communist Party, which had placed them at risk and now seemed to have forgotten them.

The reconciliation between Yugoslavia and the Soviet Union, sealed by a visit to Belgrade by the Soviet premier, did not change the situation; nor did a visit soon after by Palmiro Togliatti. Adriano Dal Pont, a Communist from Udine who had been detained since 1949, noted in his diary: 'Khrushchev is in Belgrade, Togliatti follows him in turn, the normalization of relations is evident, but we still remain inside ... We cannot figure it out. We write an exposé, no answer. Growing nervousness. Unending discussions among us. Why have we been abandoned? We have repeatedly sent messages out by way of those who returned. They brought them to the party and to our families. The families answer, the party does not.'

It was only three years later, after a second mission to Belgrade sent by the Italian Communist Party, led now by Luigi Longo, that the problem of the detained Monfalconesi was addressed. Longo told Tito: 'In your jails there are Italian Communists who ended up in them because they carried out my orders. You cannot receive me as a friend and comrade and continue to deprive these comrades of mine of their freedom.'

Some time after that, Tito saw to it that Adriano Del Pont and the last of the detained Monfalconesi were freed to return to Italy. This was on 19 October 1956.

For many years, history forgot the inflexible Monfalconesi, who had experienced the most bitter swindle. They themselves, not wanting to damage the party, maintained a self-imposed silence, faithfully sealing in the party archives the documents, testimonies, and personal accounts they had gathered during their years of imprisonment. Historians still have not found any traces of this precious testimony, and perhaps they will never find them. Almost everything, in fact, has been destroyed with the precise intention of erasing from history one of the most troubling episodes in the Julian region's complicated history. Times and circumstances were changing and the Italian Communist Party had no desire to broadcast the terrible experiences of those faithful and brave militants, experiences that reminded it of its Stalinist past – something that in the meantime had become a shameful embarrassment. It was better to bury the episode.

An Entire People Uprooted from Its Land

Yet the Communist counter-exodus, however terrible, is only a small part of the tragedy; in the larger one, a torrent of Italians were forced to flee the Julian region in the opposite direction, propelled by fear of Communism but also, and above all, by a Yugoslav terror campaign of ethnic cleansing. The exodus from Pola made a greater impression because of it was complete. The sight of an entire city packing its bags and abandoning its homes in order to preserve its national identity moved world public opinion. By that time, 150,000 Julians had already sought refuge in Italy, and many more would follow until the total reached 350,000. An entire population was abandoning its land in order to remain in its own country, where, paradoxically, when it was not considered foreign it was certainly viewed as unwanted.

The events of the 1990s that have bloodied the ex-Yugoslavia, raising waves of indignation and heartfelt cries of solidarity with the Bosnian and Kosovar refugees, victims of renewed Serbo-Croatian 'ethnic cleansing,' are bringing back to memory the similar drama lived fifty years ago by the Julian population. Yet, so far there has been no examination or self-critique of this painful episode, which for years has been deliberately forgotten. The topic is not yet considered politically correct. Italy does not have a clean conscience with regard to these unfortunate Italians, who paid the country's war debts on behalf of all Italians. Italy did not do everything possible for them. This was bluntly stated by Harold Macmillan, representative of the Allied military government, who one day told Italian leaders: 'The fault is all yours. It's you who do not want to save Venezia Giulia.'

In fact, the Trieste question was an awkward topic for all Italian governments of the time. De Gasperi would refer to it as 'a torment.' There were different and often contradictory reasons for this. To understand them today, we must remember that Italy had just come out of a disastrous war. For twenty years of Fascist dictatorship, Italy had been drunk with patriotism; after the Fascists, many Italians rejected national values in response. Any suggestion that the nation's borders ought to be defended was tagged 'Fascist throwback.' The flag-waving demonstrations in Trieste that called for the city to be reunited with the Motherland (or, rather, with the Country – even the word 'Motherland' had been discreetly replaced by this less charged synonym) were considered 'a worrying sign of resurgent Fascism.'

This is why, even though public opinion generally favoured the Julians, the major Italian political parties were reluctant to do so. The Christian Democrats, who should have represented the values of old, pre-Fascist Italy, hesitated to appropriate nationalist themes; it preferred to appeal to Catholic pacifists, who in 1915 had come out against Italian entry into the war for the sake of acquiring Trento and Trieste. The Left, for its part, was still tied to the ideals of anti-Fascist struggle and proletarian internationalism and felt uncomfortable defending the eastern borders. The Left was trapped in a sort of romantic camaraderie that pushed it toward solidarity with anyone who had fought against Fascism, and it continued to lump together the international brigades that had fought in the Spanish Civil War, the Italian partisans, and the *Titini*, seeing them all as champions in the struggle for freedom. Pietro Nenni, for example, considered himself 'an old comrade in arms with Marshal Tito from days of the international brigades in Spain.' In the meantime, Ernesto Rossi, an ideologue of the Action Party, wrote to Gaetano Salvemini that 'to fixate oneself on this Trieste, or Gorizia, or Istria question makes no sense to me. As long as we remain within the tradition of sovereign nation states these will remain insoluble questions.'

While the Christian Democrats hesitated and while the theorists of the Left hypothesized the creation of a classless and borderless society, the problem of absorbing the refugees from Venezia Giulia was becoming more and more acute. Besides the political problems, there was also a much more practical one: the economic one. The war had flattened Italy; the country had little money to spend. Generous offers of financial help came in from individual citizens and from some banks, but these could not replace state intervention. The refugees were being housed temporarily in schools and abandoned barracks and in 109 refugee centres that had been organized as best could be, here and there throughout Italy. But this was a temporary solution. What would be their future?

The government approached this question with a poorly disguised sense of annoyance and with obvious annoyance it pondered the proposal to concentrate all the Julian refugees in one single area so as to prevent their dispersion.

The idea of creating a 'second Pola' in Italy was nothing new. It had already been considered by the Julian Committee, led by the indefatigable Antonio De Berti, from Pola, a Socialist deputy since 1921, who had been imprisoned several times by the Fascists and the Nazis. It is he who was largely responsible for organizing the exodus and for compelling the government to do something for the refugees.

The project of a new Pola in Italy had already been sketched by engineers and urbanists, and was viewed favourably by the Allies. Some of the locations proposed for the new 'Julian city' were the Gargano, Fertilia in Sardinia, and the hunting reserve of Castel Porziano. This new city would enable the refugees to insert themselves into the economy of the country without losing their own identity.

Indro Montanelli wrote at the time in the *Corriere della Sera*:

The Julians did not bat an eye when they had to abandon their land, houses, and belongings. But they cannot resign themselves to being fractioned away and divided. 'As long as we are together, we are strong' they say, and I know what they are talking about. They are talking about the fear of losing, because of the incomprehension and scepticism of other people, that warmth of solidarity and that fever of Italianness that ties them all into a great family and has been the greatest wealth for which they have sacrificed all other. They do not want to draw apart. They do not want their children to grow up Lombard, or Pugliese, or Piedmontese. They want them to remain Julian even in Lombardy, in Puglia, and in Piedmont. This is understandable, it is good that it be like this.

Montanelli was a firm believer in the triumph of good sense; unfortunately, politics does not always go along with good sense. Italian politicians of the time chose instead to disperse the Julian refugees, in order to dissolve in the diaspora a thorny political problem and evade a heavy responsibility. Concentrating them in a new motherland would have nurtured a cult of memory. The proposal made by the Julian Committee was thus rejected by the government, and the refugees were dispersed not only throughout Italy, but throughout the entire world. Yet through their associations, their newsletters, and their research centres, these exites eventually succeeded in saving their cultural identity and also in conserving the precious seed of their Italianness.

Trieste, 'Berlin of the Adriatic'

In the years that followed, the Julian question remained a flash point of national and international debate. Trieste, a contested city, the 'Berlin of the Adriatic,' where the First and the Second worlds clashed, became the object of diplomatic wrangles and complex political manoeuvres. The Tripartite Declaration of 20 March 1948 was a strongly political document. In it, the United States, Great Britain, and France declared that 'the best way to meet the democratic aspirations of the people and to make peace and stability possible in the area is to return the Free Territory of Trieste to Italian sovereignty.' This declaration, which required Soviet consent in order to be put into practice, sought to influence – and certainly did influence – the election of 18 April 1948, which called on Italians to choose between Communism and democracy. Even so, it was a solemn affirmation of principle which the Italian government seized on with hope.

These hopes faded quickly when, on the following 28 June, relations between Tito and Stalin disintegrated. The Cominform resolution had reshuffled the deck. With Yugoslavia's departure from the Soviet sphere, the eastern border of Italy became less 'hot.' The Allies now softened their stance toward Belgrade, which was now a thorn in the side of the Soviet empire. Reversing their position, the Italian Communists launched a fierce media blitz against the Yugoslav 'traitors' and began a drastic cleansing of real and suspected Titoist agents from their own ranks. For its part, the Communist Party of the Free Territory of Trieste, led by Vittorio Vidali, firmly repudiated the Yugoslav line and transformed itself, in agreement with the Soviet Union, into the strongest supporter of a Free State of Trieste as proposed by the peace treaty. In this hubbub of undercover games and sudden U-turns, the Italian government continued to press for implementation of the Tripartite Declaration. In the meantime, however, the Allies had changed their strategy. They were now anxious to free themselves of a heavy burden. They declared themselves ready to give the entire Zone A to Italy, but they could not guarantee the restitution of Zone B, which had been incorporated de facto into Yugoslavia.

Debate on all this continued for several years. Some of the players recommended giving up Zone B in order to acquire Trieste and Zone A. Prime Minister Alcide De Gasperi, however, tied himself more closely to the Tripartite Declaration than even the Allies themselves, who had proclaimed it. These long and tense discussions were often interrupted by noisy demonstrations by the Triestinians, who demanded annexation with Italy. These demonstrations were harshly suppressed, with dead and wounded in the streets, by the forces of the Venezia Giulia Police under orders from the British general John T.W. Winterton, governor of the Free Territory of Trieste.

In response to these demonstrations, and anxious to find an exit from the Julian region and the Free Territory of Trieste, toward the end of 1952 the Allies added Italian political advisors to the British and American advisors, who were to share power equally with them. Later, even the administration was turned over to an Italian Chief Director, who answered directly to General Winterton.

This Allied decision did not impinge on the principle of the division of the Free Territory of Trieste; even so, Belgrade protested, accusing the Italian government of subtly annexing Zone A.

In the meantime, the international chessboard had yet again been overturned, this time by Stalin's death and the rapprochement between the Soviet Union and Yugoslavia. Marshal Tito now had friends in both the West and the East. Strengthened by this, he began once again to make demands. On 28 August 1953, in a very harsh note, a Yugoslav organ announced that Belgrade had 'lost its patience' and was planning to annex Zone B in response to 'the cold annexation of Zone A on the part of Italy.'

This threatening note angered the government in Rome, where De Gasperi had been replaced as head of government by Giuseppe Pella, an easygoing businessman from Biella whom circumstances would transform into a combative demagogue. The result was a political firestorm that was, perhaps, stronger than it had to be. It seemed that Tito was going to annex Zone B at any moment and possibly even Zone A, which the note had declared 'an integral part of Yugoslav territory.' Faced with this prospect, Pella reacted sharply. In impassioned meetings with his collaborators, he even considered military action in Zone A should Tito annex Zone B. For the first time in the history of the young Italian Republic, armed intervention to resolve a diplomatic conflict was being seriously considered. Italian troop movements along the eastern border raised fears and doubts.

To Pella's muscle flexing (the historian Mario Tascanini wrote that Pella was even ready to 'fire on the Anglo-Americans had they not let the Italians into Zone A'), Tito responded with a great popular demonstration at Oktoglica (San Basso), less than six kilometres from the border. This took place on 6 September 1953. Seventy-two trains and other transport means brought 250,000 ex-partisans and thousands of Slovenian and Croatian citizens to town. Tito delivered a very harsh speech laced with irony and disdain. In response to accusations that Yugoslavs had carried out horrendous massacres at the *foibe*, he listed the crimes attributed to the Italian occupation. He spoke of 70,000 Slovenians deported, and of 11,000 people shot, and he raised to 430,000 the total number of victims of the Italian army.

Regarding the Free Territory of Trieste, Tito sarcastically emphasized that he had no intention of seizing Zone B, for the simple reason that it was already Yugoslav territory. Then, to the thunderous applause of the immense crowd, he turned directly to Italy, a few steps away, and with threatening words defined as 'aggressions' the re-enforcement of the border posts. 'No,' Tito concluded, 'you will not occupy Zone A and so it would be best for your divisions to return to barracks and for you to start a dialogue.'

The following days were confusing, with troop movements and mutual accusations and notes of protest. Pella's expressions of national pride had agitated the *piazze* of Italy (especially in Trieste) and alarmed the political world. By moving troops on his own initiative, Pella had breached an important principle: although Italy had been a member of NATO for three years, it had moved its troops without warning its allies. This could have provoked a strong reaction within the North Atlantic Alliance. Much more worrying than an error in protocol was the possibility of military intervention, even though a direct Italo-Yugoslav clash was only a remote possibility (the ten thousand Allied soldiers stationed in Trieste would certainly have blocked it). The mere consideration of an armed conflict cooled the overheated situation. Meanwhile, Pella did not change the line he had taken. Unlike De Gasperi, who had refused to appropriate Zone A in order to prevent the Yugoslavs from doing the same with Zone B, the new Italian head of government believed that the acquisition of Zone A would not prejudice Italian claims to Zone B.

Pella answered Tito on 13 September, speaking in the Hall of the Horatii and Curiatii at the Campidoglio, in Rome, during the celebrations for the anniversary of the Roman Resistance. He indicated calmly that the problem of Trieste had to find a solution 'in line with the expectations of the national soul,' and he pointed to the Tripartite Declaration as its necessary and unrenounceable means. After alluding to the arrogance of Tito, who had not hesitated to declare that Zone B was now definitively Yugoslav, he claimed Italy's rights on the entire Free Territory of Trieste and reintroduced the old proposal of a plebiscite, noting that if Belgrade refused it, 'everyone would have to draw the obvious conclusions: the United States and Great Britain first among all.' He then concluded firmly: 'If this should not happen, and I refuse to believe it, Parliament and the Government would know how to interpret the interests of the Country and the will of the Nation.'

Clear words, but also dangerous ones. Nonetheless, they ignited the enthusiasm of those present in the hall. A journalist reports: 'The speech was greeted with roaring applause. Pella was obliged to stay in the Hall of the Horatii and Curiatii longer than expected. The Authorities went to him and congratulated him. When the Prime Minister headed towards the staircase to go downstairs and leave the palace, people tried to lead him towards the balcony so that he might answer the greeting of the crowds that has gathered in the piazza, all around the statue of Marcus Aurelius, and was calling on him, rhythmically enunciating his name: Pel-la, Pel-la.'

Despite this popular approval, Pella lacked the support of his own party, the Christian Democrats. Nonetheless, the proposal for a plebiscite gathered a lot of support – perhaps because no one considered it feasible. Only Togliatti continued to demand the independence and demilitarization of the Free Territory of Trieste, perfectly in line with what the Soviet Union was demanding.

On 8 October 1953, London and Washington took another step toward resolving the crisis when they announced their intention to hand Zone A to the Italian government. Giuseppe Pella replied that 'the eventual Italian acceptance could not in any way imply that Italy renounced its intentions on all the Free Territory of Trieste.' This declaration made Tito see red. He threatened to react militarily if Italian troops entered Trieste. And he turned to the United Nations (to which Italy did not yet belong), gaining its support and thereby blocking the Anglo-American initiative.

More tempestuous days followed. On 4 November, Pella spoke in Venice on the occasion of the anniversary of the victory. One hundred thousand people crowded Piazza San Marco. When he came to the problem of Trieste, the prime minister promised that the government would stand on guard: 'Yes, friends, be sure of it. For Italy, for its dignity, for its vital interests, this is the charge to which this government – every Italian government – will obey: be well on guard!'

While Pella harangued the crowd, news began to arrive of disorders in Trieste and violent clashes between demonstrators and the public security personnel, to whom Winterton had given emphatic instructions.

But the worst was to come the next day. This is how Giulio Cesare Re, a supporter of Pella's, summarized the events: 'On 5 November, in front of the church of Sant'Antonio Nuovo, in Trieste, the police fired on the defenceless crowd among whom groups of youths chased by the forces of public order had taken refuge: two dead and about fifty wounded. The bulletin issued that evening by Winterton made no mention of the profanation of the church. On 6 November the disorders continued: the police again fired on the demonstrators without first using tear gas bombs or water hoses. At the end of the day another four people lay dead and another fifty wounded.'

Events in Trieste provoked other debates, and the country, as usual, split in two. The Left sympathized with Yugoslavia and did not fail to see in the Trieste demonstrations 'signs of resurgent Fascism.' Strong voices rose to challenge these insinuations, but the pot continued to boil, and Istrians continued to flee.

The 'Temporary' Solution for the Triestinian Knot

The last great exodus took place between 1953 and 1955. The Anglo-American declaration of 8 October 1953 that Zone A would be given to Italy had profoundly depressed Italians still living in Zone B. Heeding popular wisdom more than Pella's assurances and those of various committees, even the most reluctant began to leave their land, even before the Memorandum of Understanding of 5 October 1954 confirmed their fears.

'Encouraged' by Slavic activists who were threatening reprisals, even the farmers, who until that moment had been the most rooted group, moved massively, just like the workers and the fishermen. Over the next four years, another 40,000 people fled. Many families became separated because, often, a son or a brother or a parent chose to remain in the hope that one day the region might be returned to Italy.

About a year had to pass after the tragic events in Trieste before the Triestinian knot could 'temporarily' be undone (this temporary solution would become final with the Treaty of Osimo). In the meantime, Giuseppe Pella, dumped by his party, had resigned, and Mario Scelba had been called by President Einaudi to form a new government. Italy was going through its usual difficult moment – unfortunately, not a rare thing. De Gasperi, tired and sick, had been cast aside (he would die on 19 August 1954). The 'Montesi scandal' was ripping the political world apart, unions were fighting with one another, the carousels of the 'Celere' were going crazy,[6] the police were shooting at workers and keeping files on them. At the same time, negotiations were continuing for the Free Territory of Trieste, even if the problem of Trieste and the drama of the refugees were not high on the list of national priorities. Under these conditions, on 5 October 1954 in London, the representatives of the United States and Great Britain signed, with the Italian ambassador Manlio Brosio and the Yugoslav ambassador Vladimir Velebit, the Memorandum of Understanding. It declared:

> As soon as the present Memorandum is initialled and the corrections to the line of demarcation stipulated by it are carried out, the governments of the United Kingdom, of the United States, and of Yugoslavia will put an end to the military government in Zones A and B of the Territory. The

---

6 The 'Celere' is a special corps of the Italian police responsible for the orderly unfolding of demonstrations and other such public events (translator's note).

governments of the United Kingdom and the United States will withdraw their armed forces from the zone north of the new demarcation line [that is, from Zone A] and will cede the administration of this zone to the Italian government. The Italian government and the Yugoslav government will immediately extend their civil administration over the zone for which they will be responsible.

The memorandum, which in theory was temporary, made no reference to the future of Zone B. On the basis of this omission, contradictory interpretations would flourish and keep the debate going for years. Bishop Santin would call the memorandum 'an injustice committed by the fighting powers.' The Treaty of Osimo, signed on 1 October 1975 by the Italian government led by Mariano Rumor, would finally nail shut the coffin on any legitimate Italian claims to Zone B. Besides determining the exodus of Italians from Zone B, the same memorandum also forced several thousand people who had thought they were safe to undertake the exodus, as we mentioned at the beginning of this book. The corrections made to the 'Morgan line' to allow Slovenia a sea outlet had given Yugoslavia about twenty villages that had previously been in Zone A.

On the morning of 26 October, while the men of the British Royal Engineers Corps were driving in the last posts of the long yellow line that marked the new border between Italy and Yugoslavia, the Bersaglieri entered the contested city of Trieste amid the waving of flags and the applause of an immense and emotional crowd (fig. 12).

Trieste was returning, for a second time, to Italy. The Italian cities of Istria and Dalmatia, however, were not returning. Neither were the 300,000 people who participated in an exodus of biblical proportions that had depopulated the Julian region of its people. What was left in those lands ripped away from Italy were only the tombs without crosses of thousands of Italians thrown into the *foibe* by a program of ethnic cleansing that, for half a century, historians and politicians have stubbornly denied.

Today, perhaps, having seen what happened in Bosnia, in Croatia, in Kosovo, they might change their minds.

Bibliography

Alessi, Rino. *Trieste viva*. Rome: Gherardo Casini, 1954.

Alexander, Harold G. *The Alexander Memoirs, 1940–1945*, ed. John North. London: Cassel, 1962. Italian ed., *Le memorie*, trans. Enzo Peru. Milan: Garzanti, 1963.

Amoretti, Gian Nicola. *La vicenda italo-croata*. Rapallo: Ipotesi, 1979.

Andreotti, Giulio. *De Gasperi e il suo tempo. Trento–Vienna–Roma*. Milan: Mondadori, 1956.

Arneri, Glauco. *Breve storia della città di Trieste*. Trieste: Lint, 1998.

Bartoli, Gianni. *Il martirologio delle genti adriatiche. Le deportazioni nella Venezia Giulia, Fiume e Dalmazia*. Trieste: n.p., 1961.

Bedeschi, Giulio. *Fronte italiano: c'ero anch'io*. Milan: Mursia, 1987.

Benco, Silvio. *Contemplazione del disordine*. Udine: D. Del Bianco, 1946. 2nd ed, with intro. by Elvio Guagnini, Turriaco: [n.p.]; Monfalcone: Savorgnan, 1999.

Bertoldi, Silvio. *Dopoguerra*. Milan: Rizzoli, 1993.

Bettiza, Enzo. *Esilio*. Milan: Mondadori, 1996.

Biso, Norberto. *I vivi, i morti e i naviganti*. Milan: Longanesi, 1996.

Bocca, Giorgio. *Storia della Repubblica Italiana: Dalla caduta del Fascismo a oggi*. Milan: Rizzoli, 1982.

Bonvicini, Guido. *Decima marinai! Decima Comandante! La fanteria di marina 1943–45*. Milan: Mursia, 1988.

Borghese, Junio Valerio. *Sea Devils*, trans. James Cleugh and adapted by the author. London: Melrose, 1952. Republished as *Sea Devils: Italian Navy Commandos in World War II*. Annapolis, MD: Naval Institute Press, 1995. Original italian, *La X flottiglia Mas*. Milan: Mursia, 1995.

Carnier, Pier Arrigo. *Lo sterminio mancato. La dominazione nazista nel Veneto orientale, 1943–1945*. Milan: Mursia, 1982.

– *L'armata cosacca in Italia, 1944–1945*. Milan: Mursia, 1990.

Chiopris, Fulvio. *Calvario adriatico*. Milan: Edizioni del Borghese, 1969.

Churchill, Winston. *The Second World War*. London: Cassell, 1964. Italian ed., *La seconda guerra mondiale*, 6 vols., trans. Olga Ceretti Borsini et al. Milan: Mondadori, 1963.

Ciano, Galeazzo. *Diary 1937–1943*. New York: Enigman Books, 2002. Italian ed., *Diario 1937–1943*. Bologna: Cappelli, 1948.

Coceani, Bruno. *Mussolini, Hitler, Tito alle porte orientali d'Italia*. Bologna: Cappelli, 1948. 2nd ed., Gorizia: Istituto Giuliano di Storia, Cultura, e Documentazione, 2002.

Cox, Goeffrey. *The Road to Trieste*. London: W. Heinemann, 1947. Republished as *The Race for Trieste*. London: W. Kimber, 1977. Italian ed., *La corsa per Trieste*. Gorizia: Goriziana, 1985.

De Castro, Diego. *La Questione di Trieste. L'azione politica e diplomatica italiana dal 1943 al 1954*. Trieste: Lint, 1981.

De Felice, Renzo. *Mussolini*. 4 vols. in 8. Turin: Einaudi, 1966.

– *Rosso e Nero*, ed. Pasquale Chessa. Milan: Baldini & Castoldi, 1995.

De Simone, Pasquale. *Dalla Conferenza della Pace la condanna all'esodo. Documenti e ricerche*. Gorizia: ANVGD 1991 (printed, 1992).

– *Gente in esilio. Testimonianze nelle pagine dell' 'Arena di Pola.'* Gorizia: ANVGD, 1992.

– *La vana battaglia per il plebiscito. Documenti e ricerche*. Gorizia: ANVGD, 1990.

Califfi, Steno. *Pola clandestina e l'esodo.*, ed. Pasquale Di Simone. [Pola]: Ed. L'Arena di Pola, 1955. Republished, Gorizia, 1988.

Deakin, Frederik W. *The Brutal Friendship: Mussolini, Hitler, and the Fall of Italian Fascism*. New York: Harper and Row, 1962. Ital. ed., *Storia della Repubblica Sociale*, trans. Renzo De Felice et al. Turin: Einaudi, 1963.

Gigliotti, Felice. *Gorizia cimitero senza croci. Cronistoria inedita dei fatti accaduti in Gorizia e circondario dall'8.9.43 al 16.9.47 e pubblicata a cura del Movimento istriano revisionista nel 1952*. Udine, 1968. 2nd ed., Gorizia: ANVGD, 1995 (printed 1996).

Goebbels, Joseph. *The Goebbels Diaries*, trans. Louis P. Lochner. London: H. Hamilton, 1948. Ital. trans., *Diario intimo*. Milan: Mondadori, 1948.

I Comunisti a Trieste. Un'identità difficile, pref. by Alessandro Natta. Rome: Editori riuniti, 1983.

Incisa di Mamerana, Ludovico. *L'Italia della luogotenenza*. Milan: Corbaccio, 1966.

Kaltenegger, Roland. *Operationszone 'Adriatisches Küstenland': der Kampf um Triest, Istrien und Fiume, 1944–45*. Graz: L. Stocker, 1993. Ital. ed. *Zona d'operazione Littorale Adriatico*. Gorizia: Libreria Editrice Goriziana, 1996.

Lamb, Richard. *War in Italy, 1943–1945: A Brutal Story*. New York: St Martin's Press, 1994. Ital. ed. *La guerra in Italia*, trans. Raffaele Petrillo. Milan: Corbaccio, 1996. 2nd ed., Milan: TEA, 2000.

La Perna, Gaetano. *Pola, Istria, Fiume 1943–1945: la lenta agonia di un lembo d'Italia*. Milan: Mursia, 1993.

Lisiani, Vladimiro. *Good Bye Trieste*. Milan: Mursia, 1964.

Mori, Anna Maria and Milani, Nelida. *Bora*. Milan: Frassinelli, 1998.

Mutarelli, Donato. *Osimo spiegato a tutti*. Milan, 1994.

Nenni, Pietro. *Diari*, ed. Giuliana Nenni and Domenico Zucaro. Milan: SugarCo, 1981–83.

Nesi, Sergio. *Decima flottiglia nostra. I mezzi d'assalto della Marina Italiana al Sud e al Nord dopo l'Armistizio*. Milan: Mursia, 1986.

Papo da Montona, Luigi. *Albo d'oro. La Venezia Giulia e la Dalmazia nell'ultimo conflitto mondiale*. 2nd ed. rev. Trieste: Unione degli Istriani, 1995.

– *L'ultima bandiera. Storia del reggimento Istria*. Gorizia: L'Arena di Pola, 1986. 2nd ed., Rome: TER, 2000.

Piazza, Bruno. *Perché gli altri non dimentichino. Un italiano a Auschwitz*. 4th ed. Milan: Feltrinelli, 1995; 1st ed., Trieste, 1980.

Pini, Giorgio. *Itinerario tragico (1943–1945)*. Milan: Omnia di Giachini, 1950.

Pisano, Giorgio. *Storie della guerra civile in Italia (1943–1945)*. Milan: FPE, 1965.

Pitamitz, Antonio. 'Tutte le verità sulle foibe' in *Storia Illustrata* nn. 306–7 (1989).

Quarantotti Gambini, Pier Antonio. *Primavera a Trieste. Con una lettera al Presidente della Repubblica e altri scritti*. Milan: Mondadori, 1967.

Ricciotti, Lazzero. *La Decima Mas*. Milan: Rizzoli, 1984.

Rocchi, Flaminio. *L'esodo dei Giuliani, Fiumani e Dalmati*. Rome: Difesa Adriatica, 1970. 4th ed. rev. *L'esodo dei 350 mila Giuliani Fiumani e Dalmati*. Rome: Difesa Adriatica, 1998.

Romano, Paola. *La questione giuliana, 1943–1947. La guerra e la diplomazia, le foibe e l'esodo*. Trieste: LINT/Unione degli Istriani, 1997.

Scotti, Giacomo. *I disertori. Le scelte dei militari italiani sul fronte jugoslavo prima dell'8 settembre*. Milan: Mursia, 1980.

– *Ventimila caduti. Gli italiani in Jugoslavia dal 1943 al 1945*. Milan: Mursia, 1970.

– *Il battaglione degli straccioni. I militari italiani nelle brigate jugoslave: 1943–1945*. Milan: Mursia, 1974.

– *Bono Taliano*. Milan: La Pietra, 1977.

– *Goli Otok. Italiani nel gulag di Tito*. 2nd ed., Trieste: Lint, 1997.

Spazzali, Roberto. *Foibe*. Trieste, 1990. Republished, with Raoul Pupo, Milan: Mondadori, 2003.

– *Venezia Giulia, lotte nazionali in una regione di frontiera*, preface by Fulvio

Salimbeni. Gorizia: Istituto Giuliano di Storia Cultura e Documentazione, 1998.

Spriano, Paolo. *Storia del Partito Comunista Italiano*. 7 vols. Turin: Einaudi, 1967–98.

Sprigge, Sylvia. *Trieste Diary. Maggio-giugno 1945*, ed. Raoul Pupo. Gorizia: Editrice Goriziana, 1989.

Talpo, Oddone. *Dalmazia, un cronaca per la storia, 1942*. Rome: Stato maggiore dell'esercito, Ufficio storico, 1990.

Tamaro, Attilio. *Due anni di storia 1943–1954*. 2 vols. Rome: G. Volpe, 1981–85. 1st ed., Rome, 1950.

Unione degli Istriani. *I sopravvissuti alle deportazioni in Jugoslavia*. Trieste, 1997.

Valdevit, Giampaolo. *Foibe, il peso del passato. Venezia Giulia, 1943–1945*. Udine: Istituto Regionale per la Storia del Movimento di Liberazione nel Friuli-Venezia Giulia, 1997.

Index